Contents

Literacy Centers
Take It To Your Seat

What's Great About This Book

Centers are a wonderful, fun way for students to practice important skills, but they can take up a lot of classroom space. The 17 centers in this book are self-contained and portable. Students may work at a desk or even on the floor using a lapboard for writing. Once you've made the centers, they're ready to use at any time.

Three Kinds of Centers

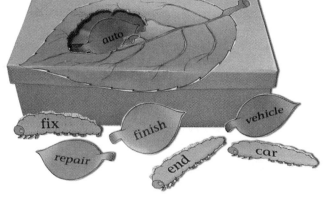

- Hanger Pocket Centers
- Shoebox Centers
- Folder Centers

Everything You Need

- Teacher direction page
    How to make the center
    Description of student task
- Full-color patterns needed to construct the center
- Reproducible task cards and blank cards for creating your own activities

Using the Centers

The centers are intended for skill practice, not to introduce skills. It is important to model the use of each center before students do the task independently.

Considering these questions in advance will avoid later confusion:

- Will students select a center or will you assign them?
- Will there be a specific block of time for centers or will the centers be used throughout the day?
- Where will you place the centers for easy access by students?
- What procedure will students use when they need help with the center tasks?
- Where will students put completed work?
- How will you track the tasks and centers completed by each student?

Hanger Pocket Centers

Hanger pocket centers can be easily stored on a hook or rod anywhere in the classroom. Students hang the center on the edge of a desk or back of a chair while working on the task.

Basic Hanger Pocket Pattern

Materials

- hanger
- 17" x 36" (43 x 91 cm) piece of paper (large brown paper bag, butcher paper, shelf paper) or fabric

Steps to Follow

Butcher paper,
shelf paper, fabric

Staple.

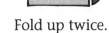

Fold up twice.

Staple.

Brown Paper Bag

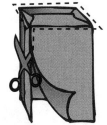

Cut up one side.
Cut out the bottom of the bag.

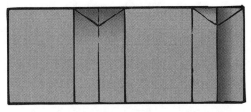

Open flat.
Attach to hanger as shown above.

Write a Letter

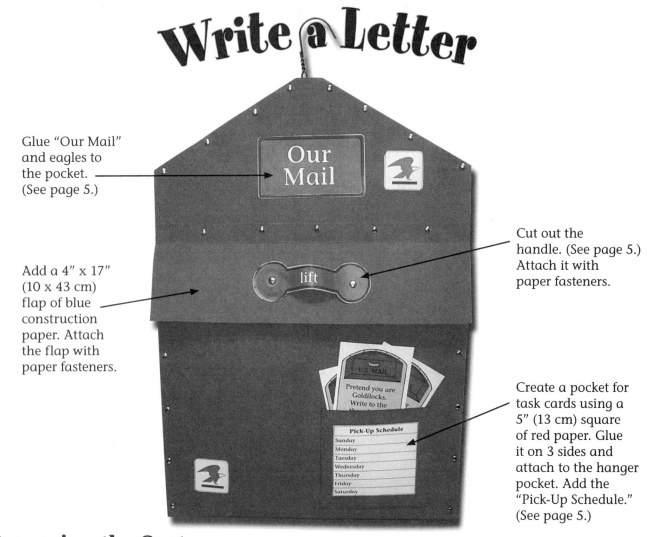

Glue "Our Mail" and eagles to the pocket. (See page 5.)

Cut out the handle. (See page 5.) Attach it with paper fasteners.

Add a 4" x 17" (10 x 43 cm) flap of blue construction paper. Attach the flap with paper fasteners.

Create a pocket for task cards using a 5" (13 cm) square of red paper. Glue it on 3 sides and attach to the hanger pocket. Add the "Pick-Up Schedule." (See page 5.)

Preparing the Center

1. Using a 17" x 38" (43 x 96.5 cm) piece of blue butcher paper, prepare the top of the basic hanger pocket following the directions on page 3. Add brass paper fasteners along the top edges.

   Fold the bottom up 14" (35.5 cm) to form a pocket. Use brass paper fasteners along the sides to form a pocket.

   Then follow the directions above to add details to the hanger pocket.

2. Laminate and cut apart the task cards on pages 7, 9, and 11 and place them in the red pocket.

3. Place a supply of writing paper in the hanger pocket. (Or provide a supply of real stationery and envelopes for students to use. Stickers make good "stamps" for these letters.)

Using the Center

1. The student takes a task card out of the mailbox hanger pocket and reads the "message." The student then writes a letter to the "person" on the task card.

2. The completed letter is put in an envelope and placed in the pocket of the "mailbox." The teacher collects the "mail" at the end of the day.

Our Mail

lift

Pick-Up Schedule

Sunday
Monday
Tuesday
Wednesday
Thursday
Friday
Saturday

6

Pretend you are
Goldilocks.
Write to the
three bears.

Write a letter
to your teacher
telling what you
like best about
school.

Pretend you got
a great gift.
Write a
thank-you note.

U.S. MAIL

Write to your
best friend.
Tell why you
like him or her.

U.S. MAIL

Write a letter to your favorite storybook character.

U.S. MAIL

Write a letter to the author of your favorite book.

U.S. MAIL

Write a letter to the principal telling how you would change the school.

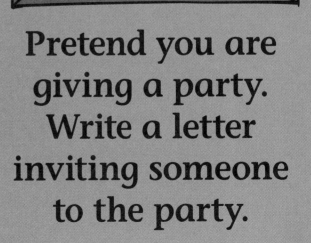

U.S. MAIL

Pretend you are giving a party. Write a letter inviting someone to the party.

U.S. MAIL

Pretend you are at summer camp. Write a letter to your parents. Tell them what you are doing.

U.S. MAIL

Write a letter to someone in your family. Tell him or her about something that you are learning to do.

U.S. MAIL

Pretend you bought a toy that was broken. Write a letter to the toy maker telling what happened. Ask for a new toy or your money back.

U.S. MAIL

Pretend you are a space alien. Write a letter about your planet to someone on Earth.

 Literacy Centers - Take It to Your Seat • EMC 788

Handwriting Practice

Cut a piece of 7" x 17" (18 x 43 cm) light brown construction paper. Cut a wavy pattern along one side. Cut the sides to the top center to form a point. Glue to the hanger pocket.

Glue a 5" x 17" (13 x 43 cm) piece of pink construction paper to the pocket. Add a 2" (5 cm) strip of brown paper.

Add "Write" with a black marking pen.

Preparing the Center

1. Using orange butcher paper, prepare the basic hanger pocket following the directions on page 3.

   Then follow the directions above to add details to the hanger pocket.

2. Laminate and cut apart the task cards on pages 15 and 17 or 19 and 21 (choose the handwriting style you teach) and place them in the pocket. Page 14 provides blank cards for your own prompts. (If your students are ready to practice cursive writing, use the blank cards to make a set of cursive practice cards for the center.)

3. Provide a supply of writing paper for students to use.

Using the Center

1. The student takes a task card out of the pencil pocket and selects a piece of writing paper.

2. The student then copies the content of the card (sentence, paragraph, poem) in his or her best handwriting.

3. The student then illustrates the writing assignment (a small picture, a colorful border, etc.).

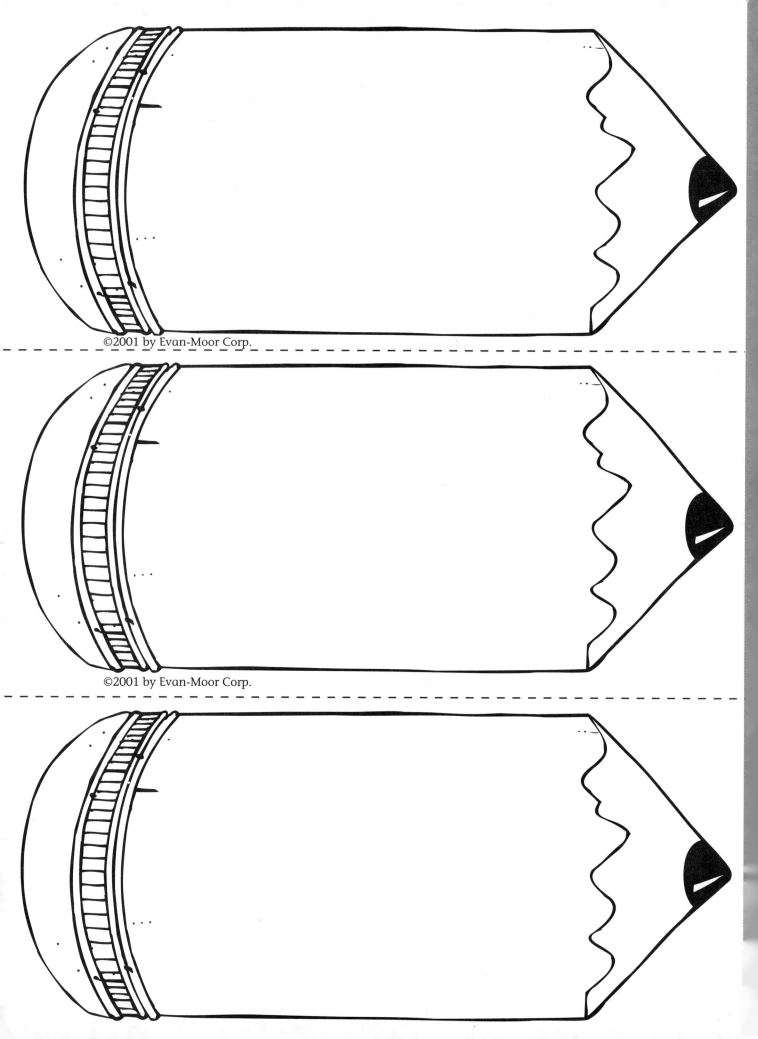

Copy this in your best handwriting.

a b c d e f g h i
j k l m n o p q r
s t u v w x y z

Now write your name in
your best handwriting.

Copy this in your best handwriting.

The quick brown fox
jumps over the lazy dog.

Now draw a fox jumping over a dog.

Copy this in your best handwriting.

Sister Susie sells small
seashells by the seashore.

Now draw yourself at the seashore.

Copy this in your best handwriting.

Jack be nimble.
Jack be quick.
Jack jump over the candlestick.

Now draw a picture about the poem.

Copy this in your best handwriting.

January	May	September
February	June	October
March	July	November
April	August	December

On your paper, circle the month
in which you were born.

Copy this in your best handwriting.

Alex jumped on his purple
and yellow skateboard.
Quick as a wink, he
zoomed down the avenue.

Now draw Alex's skateboard.

Copy this in your best handwriting.

abcdefghi
jklmnopqr
stuvwxyz

Now write your name in
your best handwriting.

Copy this in your best handwriting.

The quick brown fox
jumps over the lazy dog.

Now draw a fox jumping over a dog.

Copy this in your best handwriting.

Sister Susie sells small
seashells by the seashore.

Now draw yourself at the seashore.

Copy this in your best handwriting.

Jack be nimble.
Jack be quick.
Jack jump over the
candlestick.

Now draw a picture about the poem.

Copy this in your best handwriting.

January	May	September
February	June	October
March	July	November
April	August	December

On your paper, circle the month
in which you were born.

Copy this in your best handwriting.

Alex jumped on his purple
and yellow skateboard.
Quick as a wink, he
zoomed down the avenue.

Now draw Alex's skateboard.

Write a Story

Cut hair from two pieces of 6" x 9" (15 x 23 cm) orange construction paper.

Cut a nose from a 3" (7.5 cm) square of orange construction paper.

Cut the mouth from a 6" x 8" (15 x 20 cm) piece of red construction paper.

Glue on "wiggle eyes."

Add a ruffle cut from a 6" x 17" (15 x 43 cm) piece of blue construction paper.

Preparing the Center

1. Using brown butcher paper, prepare the basic hanger pocket following the directions on page 3.

   Then follow the directions above to add details to the hanger pocket.

2. Laminate and cut apart the cards containing writing prompts on pages 25, 27, and 29 and place them in the pocket. (Page 24 provides blank cards for your own prompts.)

3. Provide a variety of kinds of writing paper for students to use.

Using the Center

1. The student selects a writing prompt from the clown, reads it, and writes a story.

2. The student then illustrates the story in some way (a picture, a border, etc.).

Mark,
If I were in the circus, I would be a clown. I would make people laugh when I

If I were in the circus,

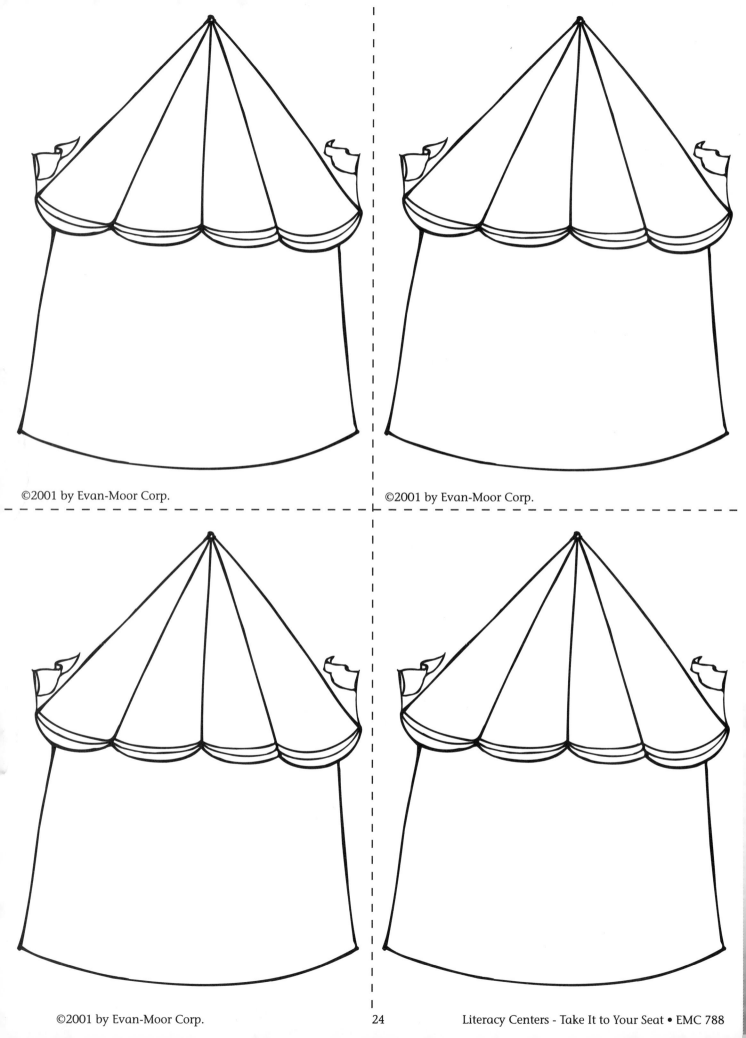

Literacy Centers - Take It to Your Seat • EMC 788

If I were in the circus, I would be...

It made me smile to see the clowns...

Ten dogs got out of a small car and...

I saw a tiger...

Literacy Centers - Take It to Your Seat • EMC 788

Ben's dad is an animal trainer for the circus.

The circus train broke down and the animals escaped.

How can I earn money to buy a ticket to the circus?

The best part of going to the circus is...

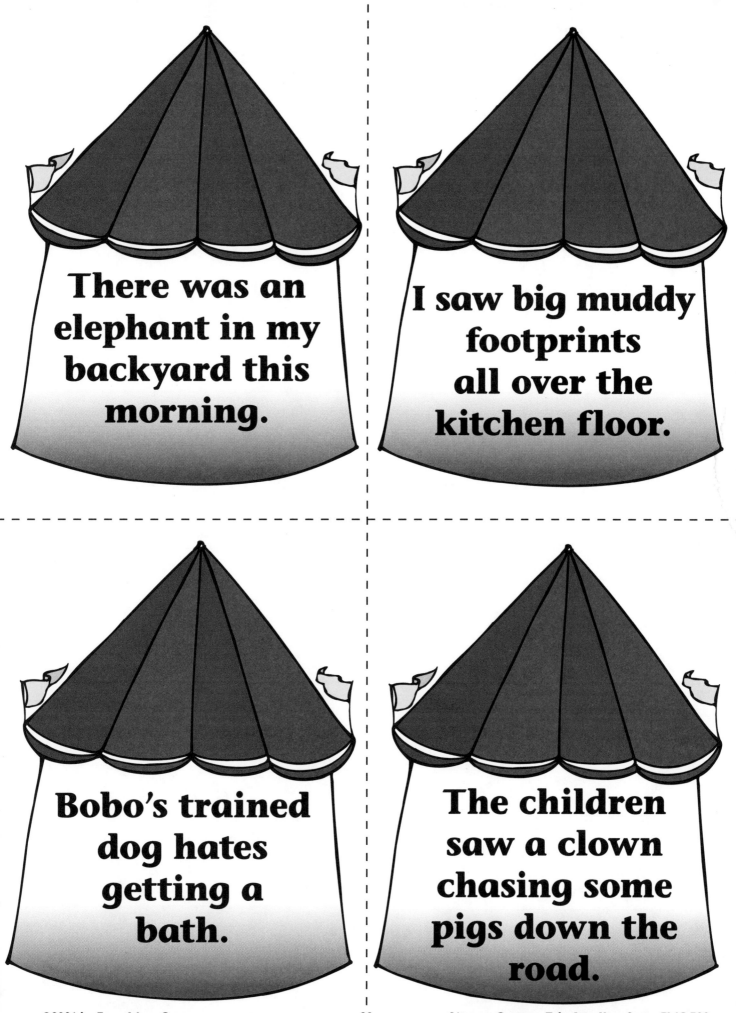

There was an elephant in my backyard this morning.

I saw big muddy footprints all over the kitchen floor.

Bobo's trained dog hates getting a bath.

The children saw a clown chasing some pigs down the road.

Read a Poem

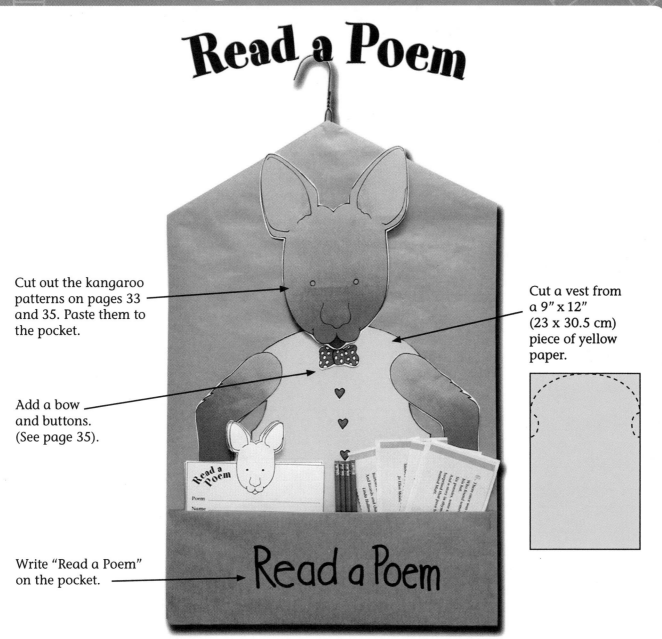

Cut out the kangaroo patterns on pages 33 and 35. Paste them to the pocket.

Add a bow and buttons. (See page 35).

Write "Read a Poem" on the pocket.

Cut a vest from a 9" x 12" (23 x 30.5 cm) piece of yellow paper.

Preparing the Center

1. Using blue butcher paper, prepare the basic hanger pocket following the directions on page 3.

   Then follow the directions above to add details to the hanger pocket.

2. Laminate and cut apart the poem cards on pages 37, 39, and 41 and place them in the pocket.

3. Reproduce a supply of answer forms (page 32).

Using the Center

1. The student takes a task card out of the pocket and reads the poem.

2. The student then writes the number of the card on the answer form and answers the questions about the poem.

Read a Poem

Poem number _____

Name _____

1. _____

_____

_____

2. _____

_____

_____

3. _____

_____

_____

Literacy Centers - Take It to Your Seat • EMC 788

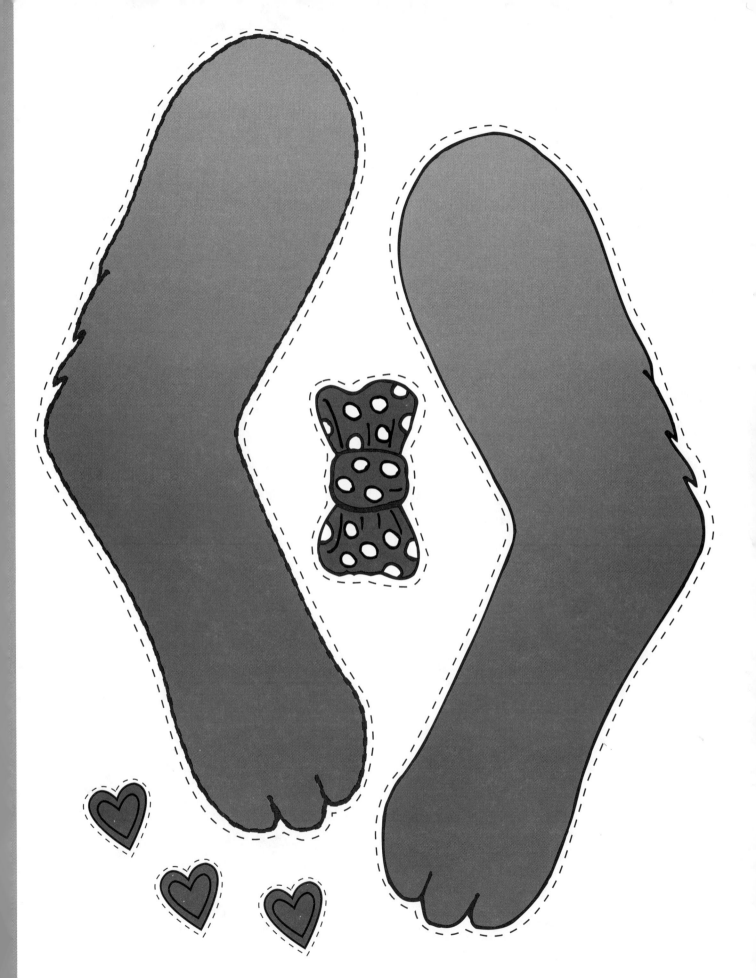

1. Buzz, Buzz, yellow bee
Have you any honey?
Yes sir, yes sir.
I sell it for money.
1 jar for a nickel,
2 jars for a dime.
Come along and
Buy some anytime.

Jo Ellen Moore

1. What does the bee sell?
2. How much does the honey cost?
3. Where do you think the bee gets the honey to sell?

---

2. It's an insect
not a spider.
It has six legs
instead of eight.

Three on this side,
three on that side,
and it's crawling
on my plate.

*Karen Adler and
Andra Christenson*

1. How is an insect different from a spider?
2. Where is the insect?
3. How would you feel if you saw an insect in your food?

---

3. Little Miss Muffet
Sat on a tuffet
Eating her curds and whey.
Along came a spider
Who sat down beside her
And frightened
Miss Muffet away.

Nursery Rhyme

1. What do you do with a tuffet?
2. What frightened Miss Muffet?
3. What was Miss Muffet eating?

4. Little Boy Blue
Come blow your horn.
The sheep are in the meadow.
The cows are in the corn.
Where is the little boy
That looks after the sheep?
He's under the haystack, fast asleep.

Nursery Rhyme

1. What was Little Boy Blue's job?
2. How do you know he was not doing his job?
3. Why should he blow his horn?

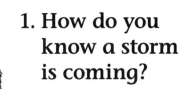

5. Clouds are boiling.
The sky is gray.
There's going to be
A storm today.

Grab your raincoat
And umbrella, too.
Before you're soaked
All through and through.

Jill Norris

1. How do you know a storm is coming?
2. What do you need to keep you dry?
3. What words rhyme in this poem?

6. There once was a boy named Matt
Who found something strange in his hat.
   Six pennies, some slime.
   And a story in rhyme,
Surprised that poor boy named Matt.

Jo Ellen Moore

1. List the strange things Matt found in his hat.
2. How did Matt feel when he looked in his hat?
3. What would you find if you looked in your hat?

7. Small and furry, little bat,
fly through the sky at night.
Listen, listen, little bat,
as echoes guide your flight.
Swoop and dive, little bat,
catch insects as you fly.
Hurry, hurry, little bat,
back to your cave nearby.

Jo Ellen Moore

1. Which words tell what the bat looks like?
2. What does the little bat eat?
3. How does the little bat find its way around?

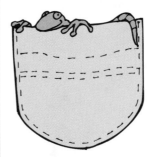

8. Pockets are nifty.
Pockets are keen.
I like them in jackets.
I like them in jeans.

They hold lots of neat stuff
I find on my walk;
Buttons and turtles
And lizards and chalk.

Linda Holliman

1. Why does the poem's writer think pockets are nifty?
2. What did she find on her walk?
3. What are you wearing that has pockets?

9. White lace
Lightly floating
Down toward the earth
Shining frosting for winter trees
Snowflakes

Jo Ellen Moore

1. Why do the winter trees look like they are covered in frosting?
2. What does "white lace" mean in the poem?
3. What do you think snowflakes look like?

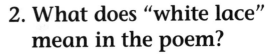

Categories

Cut ears from a 5" x 16" (13 x 40.5 cm) piece of black paper. Glue them to the back of the pocket and fold to the front.

Glue on "wiggle" eyes.

Cut a nose from a 2½" x 3" (6 x 7.5 cm) piece of pink paper.

Add a mouth with a black marking pen.

Cut a "bone" from a 5" x 17" (13 x 43 cm) piece of yellow construction paper. Glue it to the flap.

Write "Categories" on the flap.

Preparing the Center

1. Using a brown paper bag or brown butcher paper, prepare the basic hanger pocket following the directions on page 3.

   Then follow the directions above to add details to the hanger pocket.

2. Make a sorting board using a sheet of 9" x 12" (23 x 30.5 cm) tagboard. Divide it into three sections labeled "Set 1," "Set 2," and "Set 3."

3. Laminate and cut apart the sorting cards on pages 45, 47, 49, 51, and 53. Place each set of sorting cards in a separate envelope. Glue the directions to the outside of the envelope.

4. Reproduce a supply of answer forms (page 44).

Set 1	Set 2	Set 3

Name_____ Card Set_____

set name	set name	set name
1._____	1._____	1._____
2._____	2._____	2._____
3._____	3._____	3._____
4._____	4._____	4._____
5._____	5._____	5._____

Using the Center

1. The student selects an envelope and reads the directions. Using the sorting board, the student places each card in the correct set.

2. The student writes the name of the set and the items belonging in each set on the answer form.

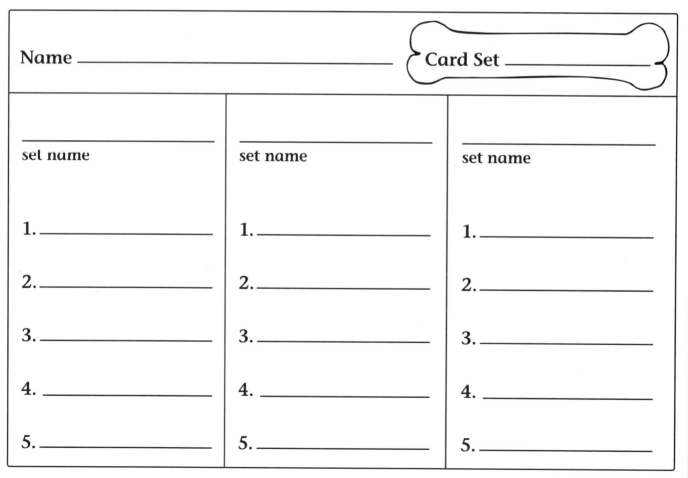

Name —————————————————————— **Card Set** —————————

set name	set name	set name
1.—————	1.—————	1.—————
2.—————	2.—————	2.—————
3.—————	3.—————	3.—————
4.—————	4.—————	4.—————
5.—————	5.—————	5.—————

Name —————————————————————— **Card Set** —————————

set name	set name	set name
1.—————	1.—————	1.—————
2.—————	2.—————	2.—————
3.—————	3.—————	3.—————
4.—————	4.—————	4.—————
5.—————	5.—————	5.—————

2 Sort the vehicle cards into these sets:

land   air   water

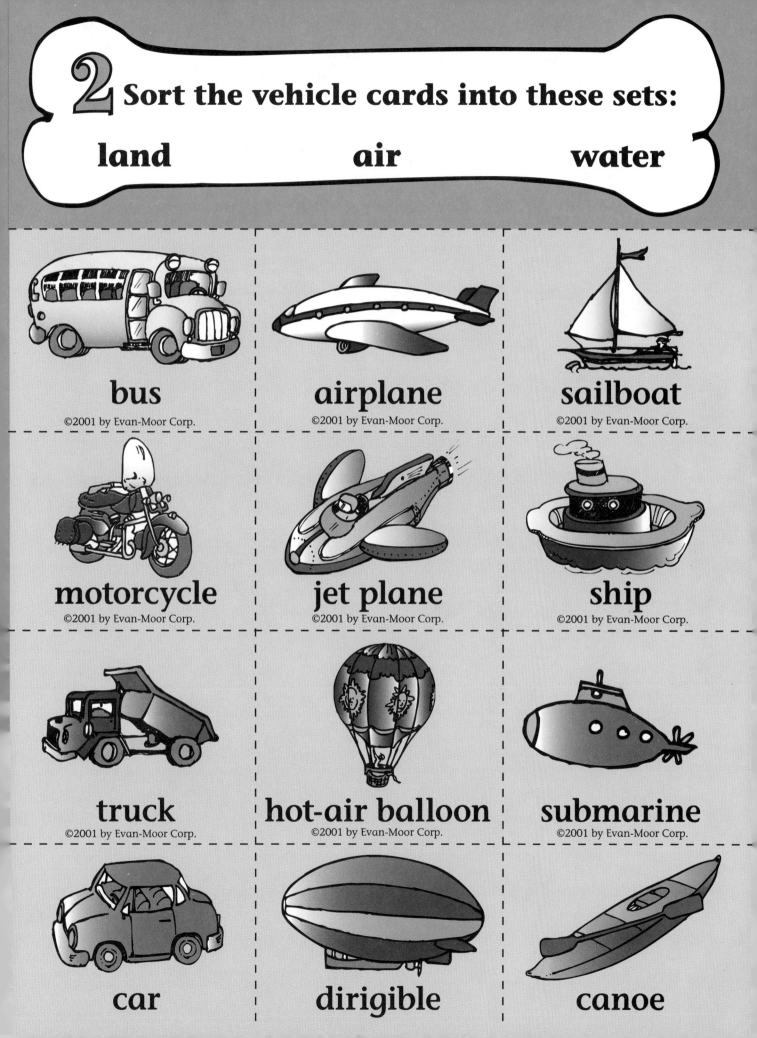

bus

airplane

sailboat

motorcycle

jet plane

ship

truck

hot-air balloon

submarine

car

dirigible

canoe

Bill	**orange**	**eight**
©2001 by Evan-Moor Corp.	©2001 by Evan-Moor Corp.	©2001 by Evan-Moor Corp.
Ann	**gray**	**zero**
©2001 by Evan-Moor Corp.	©2001 by Evan-Moor Corp.	©2001 by Evan-Moor Corp.
Carlos	**purple**	**two**
©2001 by Evan-Moor Corp.	©2001 by Evan-Moor Corp.	©2001 by Evan-Moor Corp.
Jamal	**brown**	**four**
©2001 by Evan-Moor Corp.	©2001 by Evan-Moor Corp.	©2001 by Evan-Moor Corp.
Sammy	**pink**	**one**

4 Sort the word cards into these sets:

Who?　　　　When?　　　　Where?

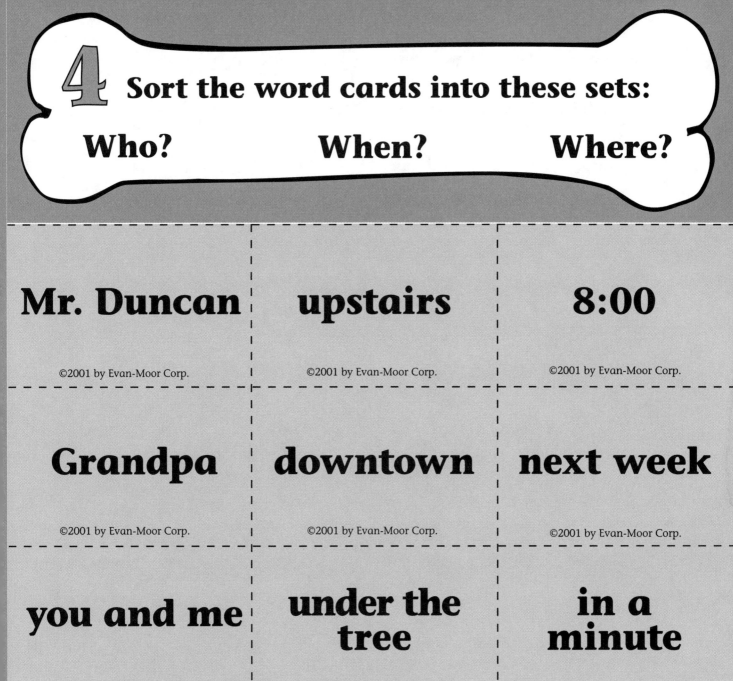

Mr. Duncan	**upstairs**	**8:00**
©2001 by Evan-Moor Corp.	©2001 by Evan-Moor Corp.	©2001 by Evan-Moor Corp.
Grandpa	**downtown**	**next week**
©2001 by Evan-Moor Corp.	©2001 by Evan-Moor Corp.	©2001 by Evan-Moor Corp.
you and me	**under the tree**	**in a minute**
©2001 by Evan-Moor Corp.	©2001 by Evan-Moor Corp.	©2001 by Evan-Moor Corp.
Uncle Bob	**in that jar**	**May 3**
©2001 by Evan-Moor Corp.	©2001 by Evan-Moor Corp.	©2001 by Evan-Moor Corp.
teacher	**New York**	**yesterday**

parents

©2001 by Evan-Moor Corp.

France

©2001 by Evan-Moor Corp.

feet

©2001 by Evan-Moor Corp.

artist

©2001 by Evan-Moor Corp.

Canada

©2001 by Evan-Moor Corp.

table

©2001 by Evan-Moor Corp.

child

©2001 by Evan-Moor Corp.

U.S.A.

©2001 by Evan-Moor Corp.

pencil

©2001 by Evan-Moor Corp.

Maria

©2001 by Evan-Moor Corp.

Spain

©2001 by Evan-Moor Corp.

box

©2001 by Evan-Moor Corp.

soldier

New
Zealand

car

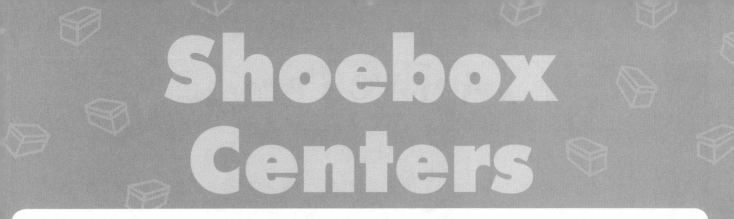

Shoebox Centers

Shoebox centers are easily stored on a table or shelf in the classroom. Students take the centers to their seats to complete a task.

Preparing a Shoebox Center

Materials

- shoebox
- Con-Tact® paper or butcher paper to fit the box
- copies of patterns provided for each center
- scissors
- craft knife
- double-sided tape
- crayons or marking pens

Steps to Follow

1. Cover the shoebox and lid with Con-Tact® paper or butcher paper. Tape the lid to the bottom of the box.

2. Laminate and cut out the pattern pieces. Tape them to the shoebox as shown for each center.

3. Cut an opening in the top of the shoebox as indicated for each center.

4. Laminate and cut out the task cards. Place them in the shoebox. Each center includes blank forms for tasks of your own choosing.

5. Paper and other materials needed are listed in the directions for each center. Special pencils or erasers for the center themes would be an added motivation.

Descriptive Paragraphs

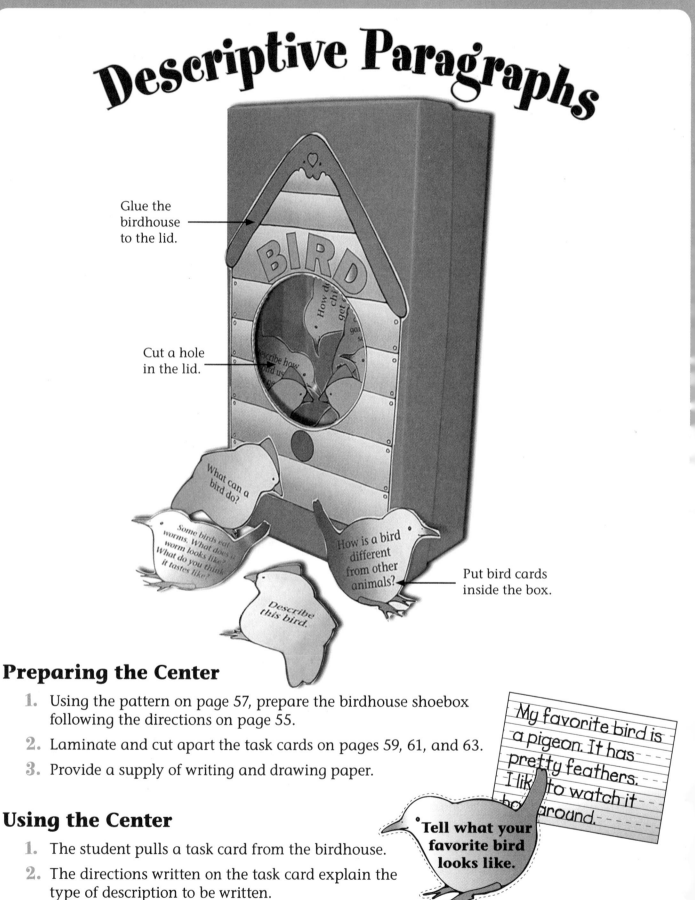

Glue the birdhouse to the lid.

Cut a hole in the lid.

Put bird cards inside the box.

What can a bird do?

Some birds eat worms. What does a worm looks like? What do you think it tastes like?

How is a bird different from other animals?

Describe this bird.

Preparing the Center

1. Using the pattern on page 57, prepare the birdhouse shoebox following the directions on page 55.

2. Laminate and cut apart the task cards on pages 59, 61, and 63.

3. Provide a supply of writing and drawing paper.

Using the Center

1. The student pulls a task card from the birdhouse.

2. The directions written on the task card explain the type of description to be written.

My favorite bird is a pigeon. It has pretty feathers. I like to watch it hop around.

Tell what your favorite bird looks like.

57

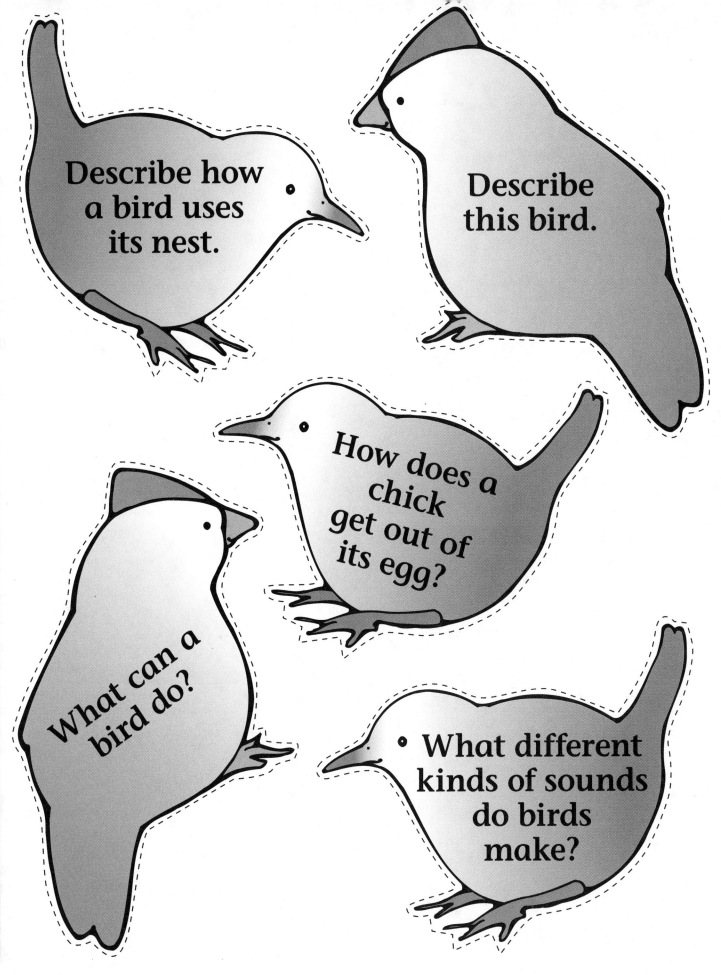

Describe how a bird uses its nest.

Describe this bird.

How does a chick get out of its egg?

What can a bird do?

What different kinds of sounds do birds make?

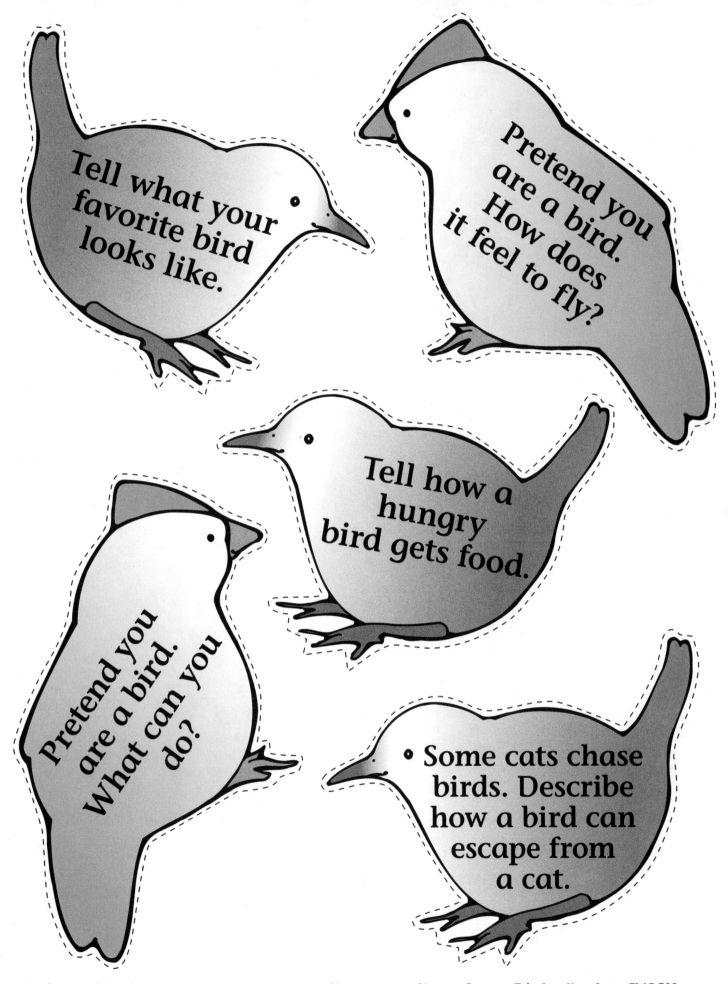

How is a bird different from other animals?

Describe how a bird takes care of its babies.

Pretend you are a bird flying over the school. Describe what you would see.

Pretend crows are eating your garden. Describe a scarecrow that will keep the crows away.

Some birds eat worms. What does a worm look like? What do you think it tastes like?

Support the Topic Sentence

Cut a hole in the lid.

Glue the bear to the box top.

Put fish cards inside the box.

I am like a bear in some ways.

Let me tell you

A bear is a mammal.

Bears live all over the world.

Bears can be dangerous.

Wild bears catch their food.

Preparing the Center

1. Using the pattern on page 67, prepare the bear shoebox following the directions on page 55.

2. Laminate and cut out the task cards on pages 69, 71, and 73. (Page 66 provides blank cards for your own tasks.)

3. Provide a supply of writing and drawing paper.

Using the Center

1. The student pulls a fish task card out of the bear shoebox.

2. The student:

   • reads the topic sentence
   • thinks about supporting information that goes with the sentence
   • copies the topic sentence on a piece of paper
   • writes one or more supporting sentences
   • draws a picture illustrating the completed paragraph

Bears and fish are very different.
Fish have scales.
Bears have fur.

Bears and fish are very different.

Literacy Centers - Take It to Your Seat • EMC 788

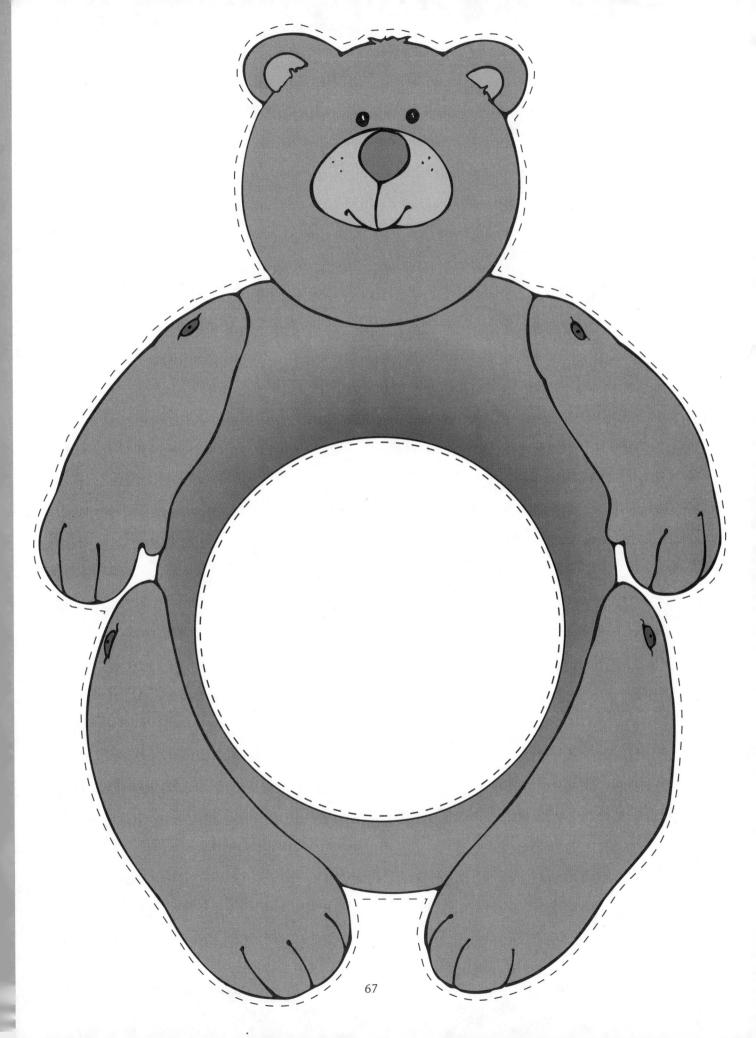

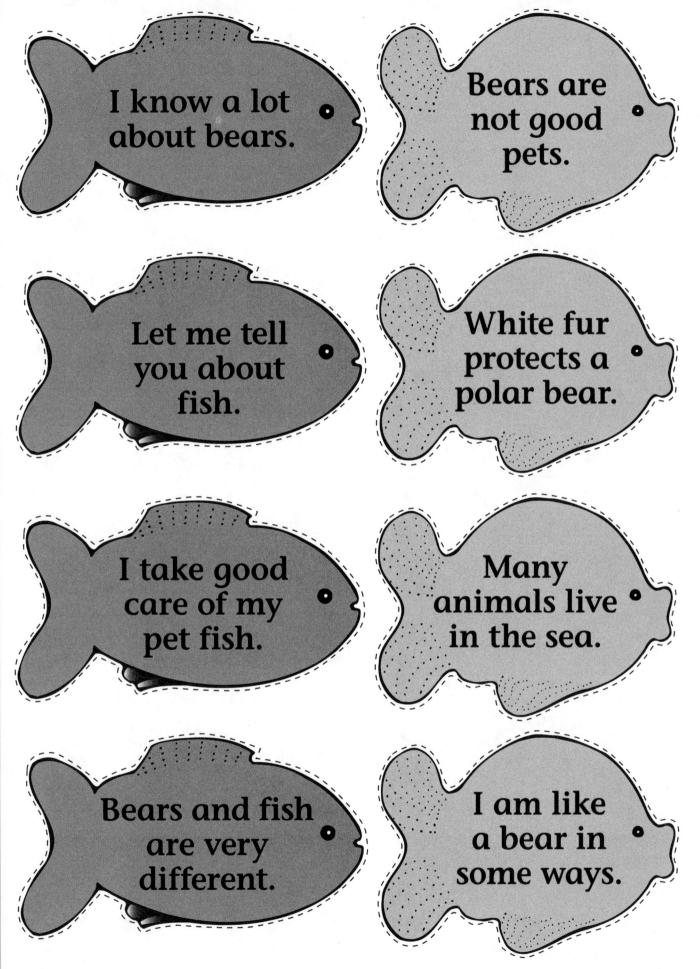

I know a lot about bears.

Bears are not good pets.

Let me tell you about fish.

White fur protects a polar bear.

I take good care of my pet fish.

Many animals live in the sea.

Bears and fish are very different.

I am like a bear in some ways.

Literacy Centers - Take It to Your Seat • EMC 788

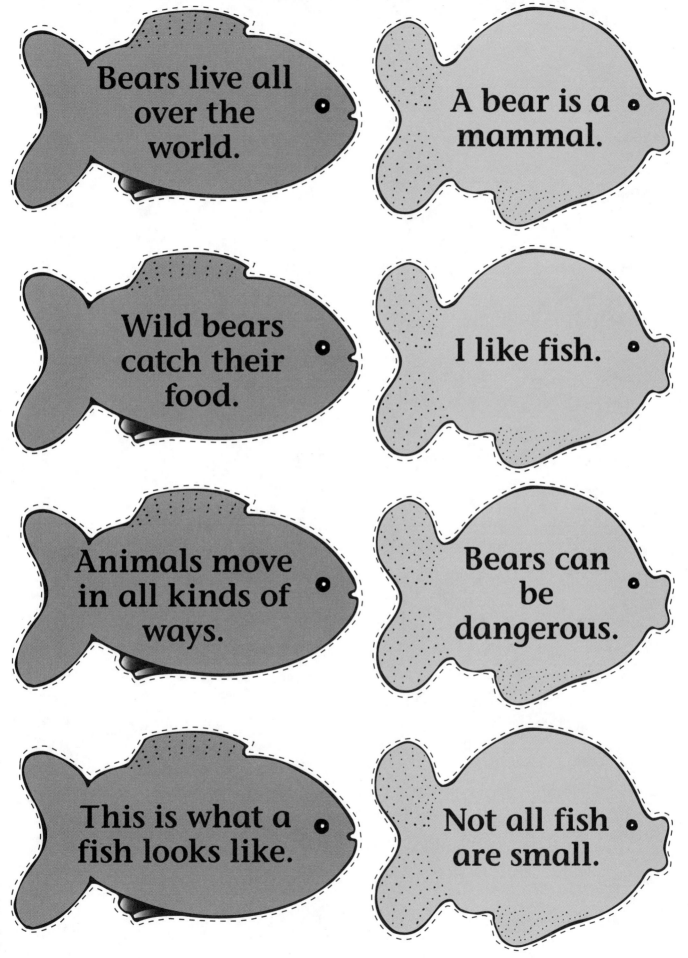

Bears live all over the world.

A bear is a mammal.

Wild bears catch their food.

I like fish.

Animals move in all kinds of ways.

Bears can be dangerous.

This is what a fish looks like.

Not all fish are small.

I would (would not) like to live in the sea.

I saw a strange animal at the zoo.

Bears and fish are the same in some ways.

I think bears should (should not) be kept in a zoo.

I would (would not) like a fish for a pet.

I am like a fish in some ways.

Fish are not the only animals with scales.

This is what a bear looks like.

Literacy Centers - Take It to Your Seat • EMC 788

Literacy Centers - Take It to Your Seat • EMC 788

Riddles

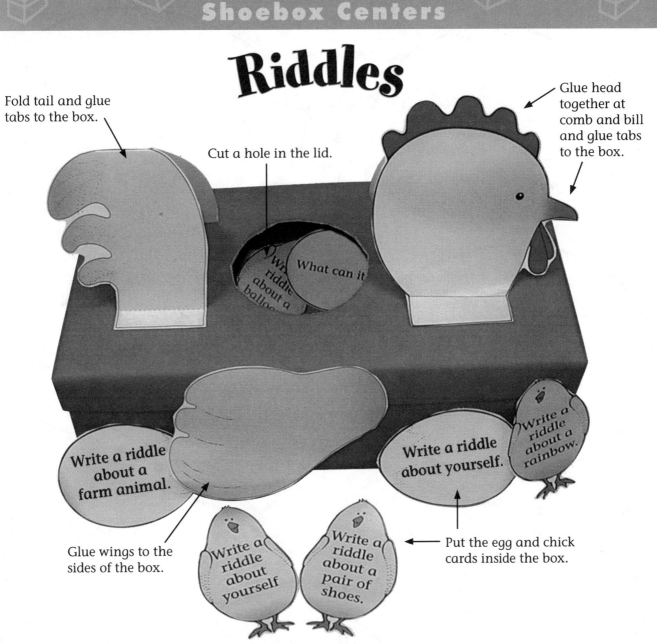

Fold tail and glue tabs to the box.

Cut a hole in the lid.

Glue head together at comb and bill and glue tabs to the box.

What can it...

Write a riddle about a balloon...

Write a riddle about a farm animal.

Write a riddle about yourself.

Write a riddle about a rainbow.

Glue wings to the sides of the box.

Write a riddle about yourself

Write a riddle about a pair of shoes.

Put the egg and chick cards inside the box.

Write a riddle about a chicken.

Write a riddle about yourself.

Preparing the Center

1. Using the patterns on pages 77 and 79, prepare the shoebox following the directions on page 55. Cut a hole in the center of the shoebox lid.

2. Laminate and cut out the task cards on pages 81 and 83. (Page 76 provides blank cards for your own tasks.)

3. Provide a supply of writing and drawing paper.

Using the Center

1. The student selects a chick or an egg from the chicken shoebox.

2. The student must write a riddle about the subject.

3. The student then draws the answer to the riddle on the back of the paper on which the riddle is written.

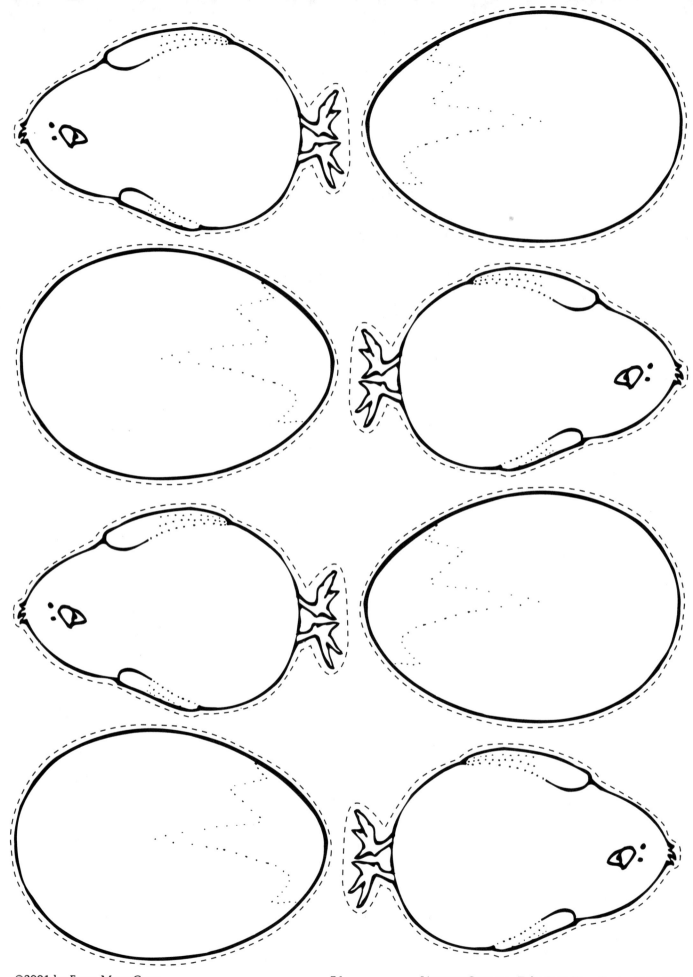

76

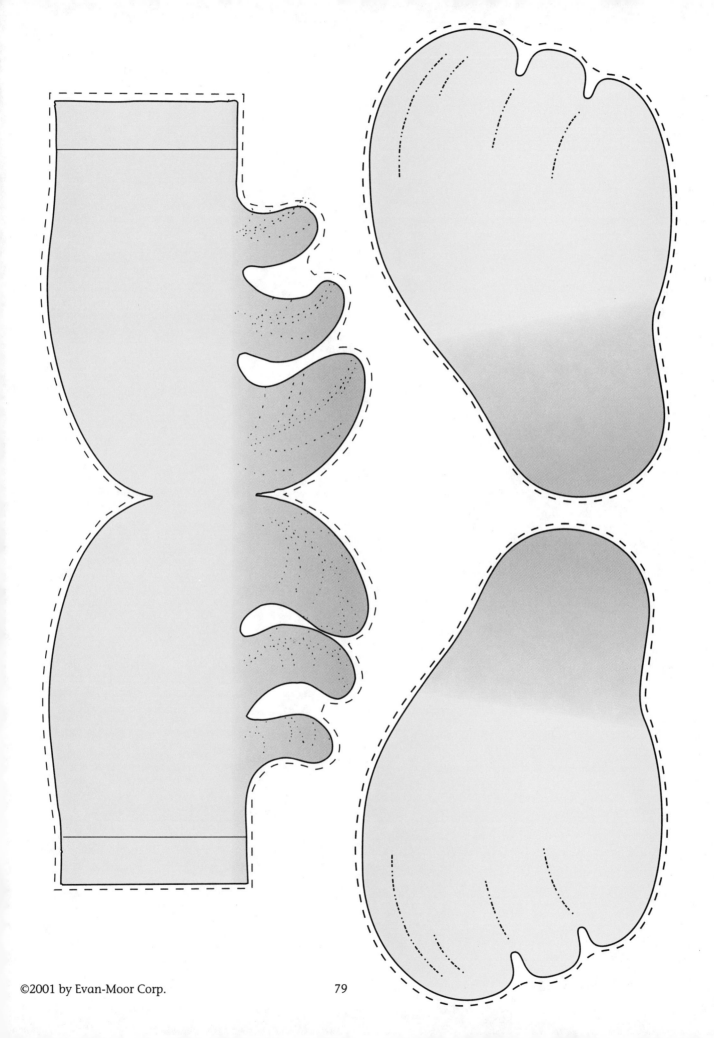

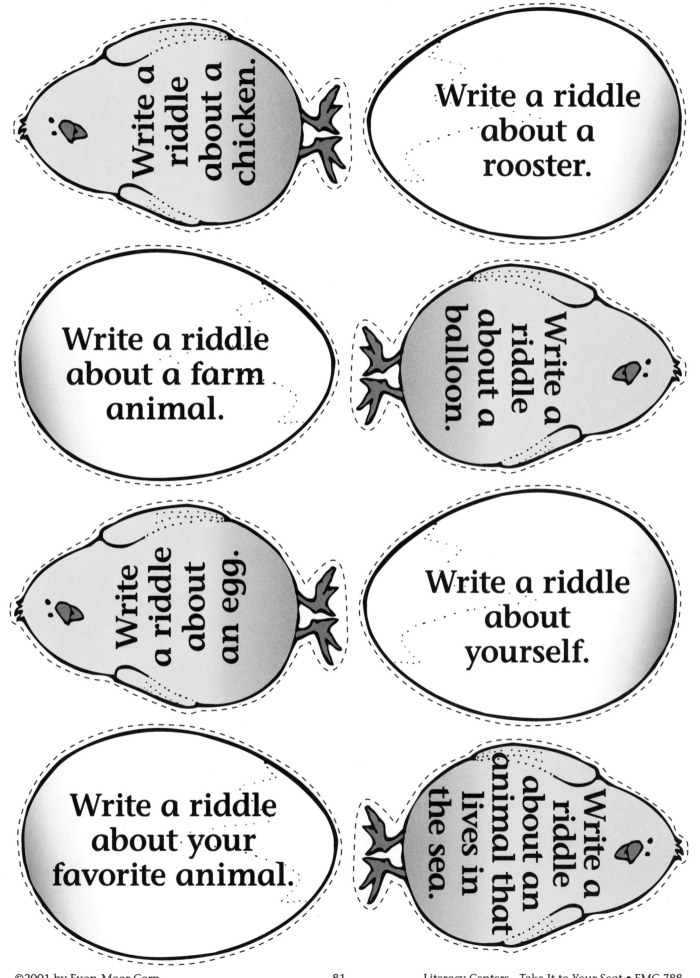

Write a riddle about a chicken.

Write a riddle about a rooster.

Write a riddle about a farm animal.

Write a riddle about a balloon.

Write a riddle about an egg.

Write a riddle about yourself.

Write a riddle about your favorite animal.

Write a riddle about an animal that lives in the sea.

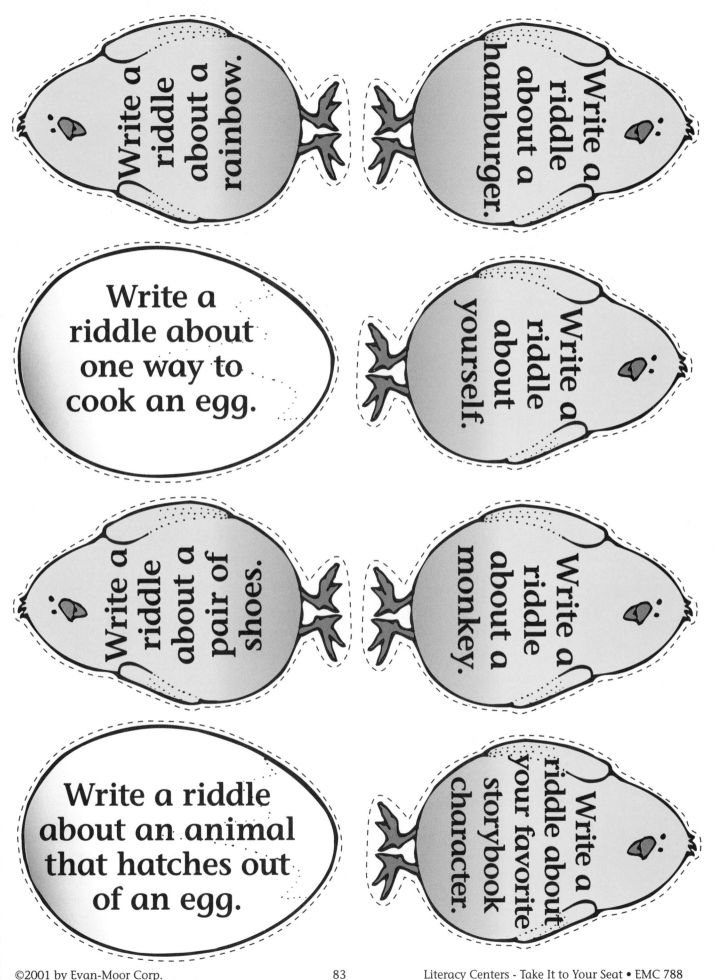

Write a riddle about a rainbow.

Write a riddle about a hamburger.

Write a riddle about one way to cook an egg.

Write a riddle about yourself.

Write a riddle about a pair of shoes.

Write a riddle about a monkey.

Write a riddle about an animal that hatches out of an egg.

Write a riddle about your favorite storybook character.

Compound Words

Glue the head to the top of the box.

Cut a flap in the box lid.

Attach peanut bag to the flap.

Glue feet on each side of the flap.

Put peanut halves inside the box.

Preparing the Center

1. Using the patterns on pages 87 and 89, prepare the shoebox following the directions on page 55.

2. Laminate and cut out the task cards on pages 91, 93, and 95.

3. Reproduce a supply of answer forms on page 86. Place them next to the shoebox.

Using the Center

1. The student takes the cards from the elephant shoebox.

2. The student:

   • matches two peanut halves to make compound words

   • writes the compound words on the answer form

Name _____ # Compound Words

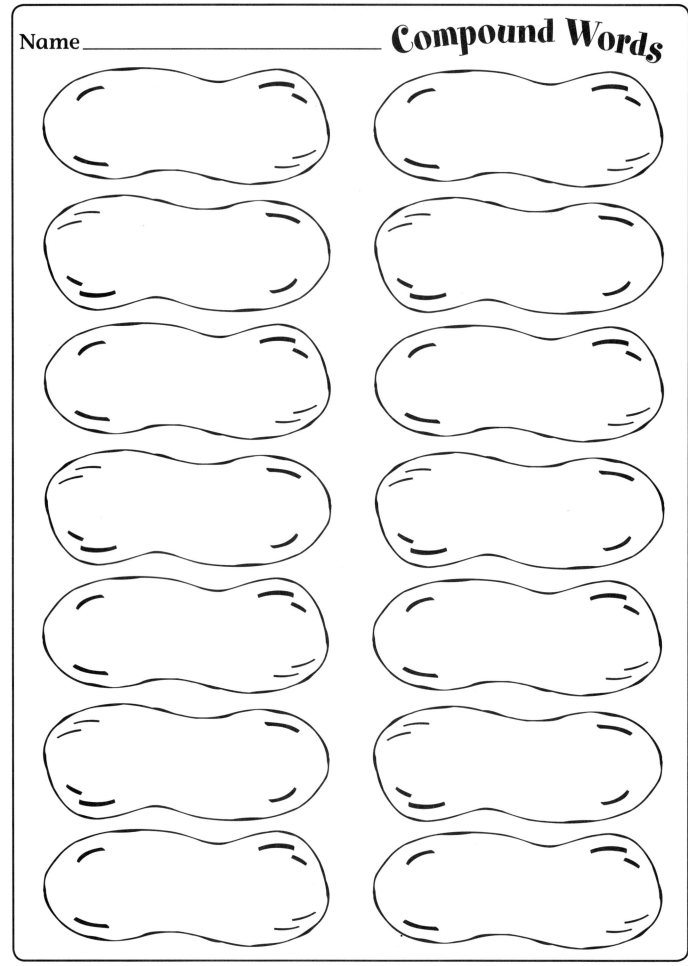

87

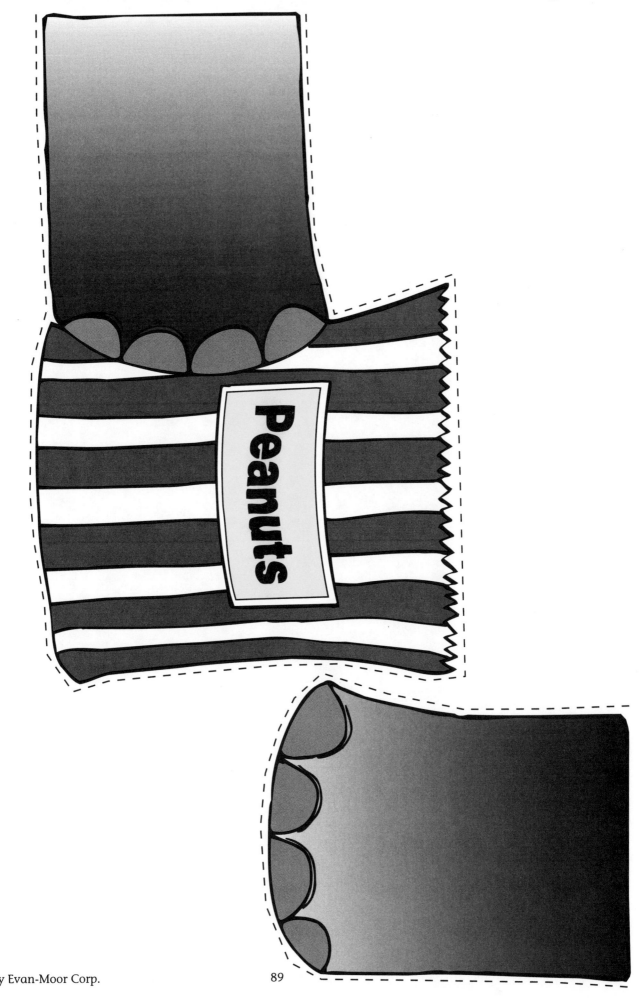

Peanuts

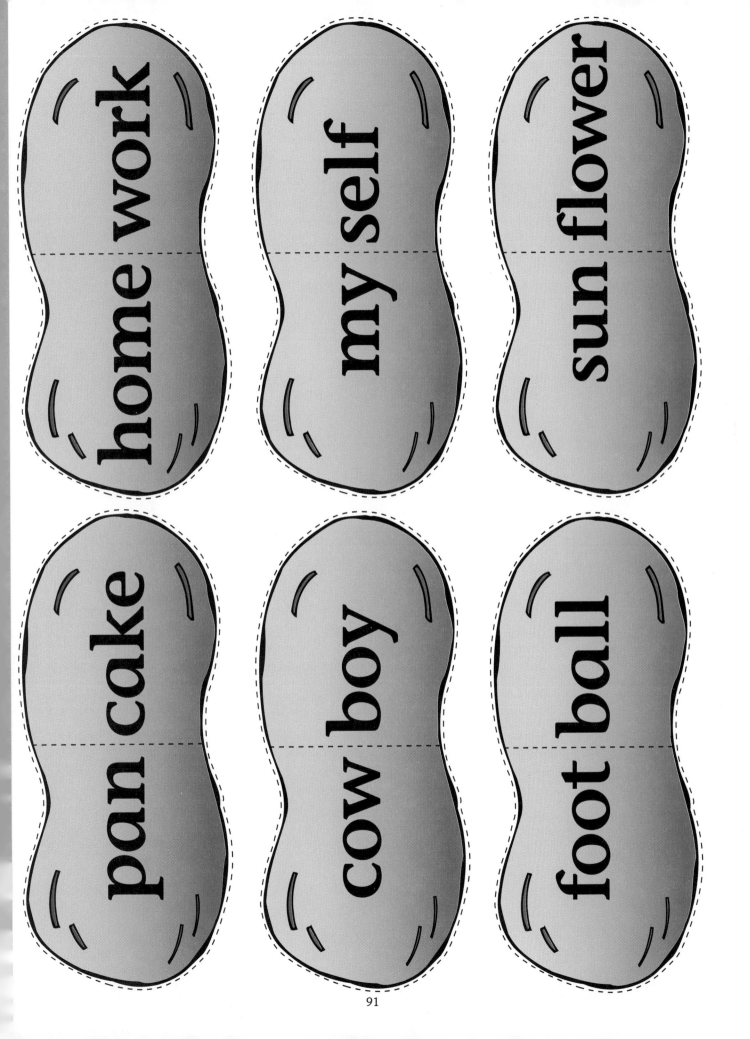

home work

my self

sun flower

pan cake

cow boy

foot ball

91

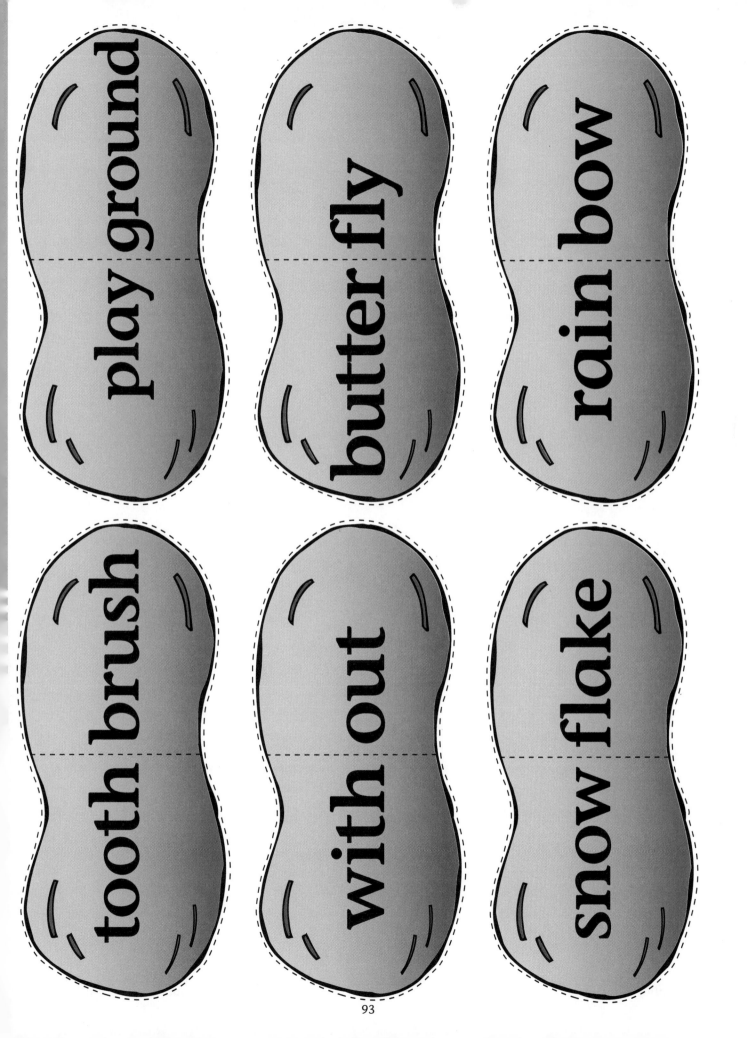

play ground

butter fly

rain bow

tooth brush

with out

snow flake

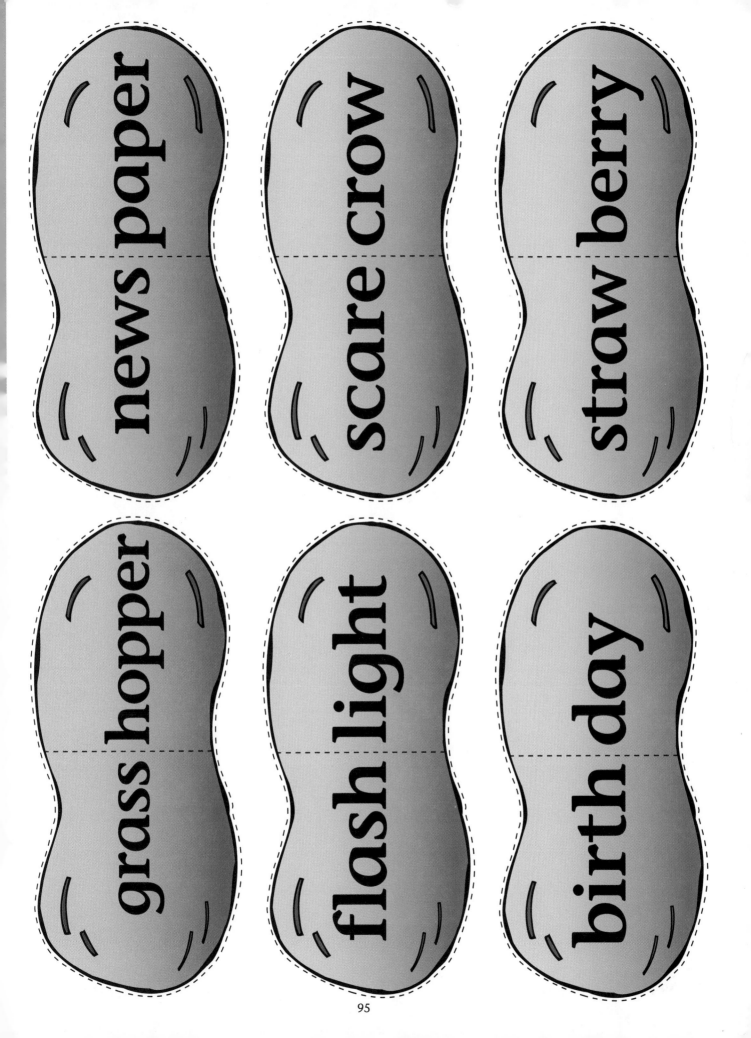

news paper

scare crow

straw berry

grass hopper

flash light

birth day

Synonyms

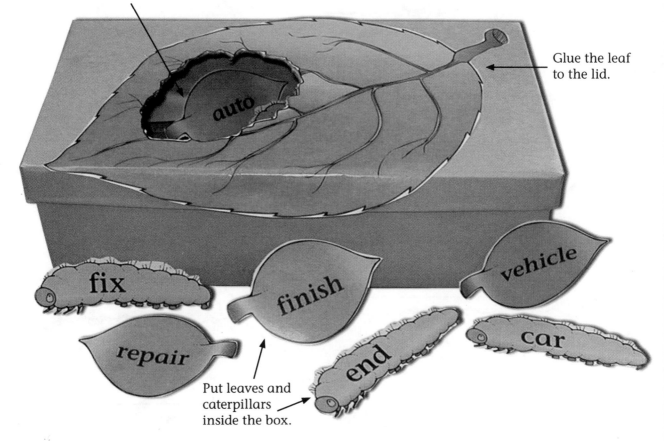

Cut a hole in the lid.

Glue the leaf to the lid.

auto

fix

finish

repair

vehicle

end

car

Put leaves and caterpillars inside the box.

Preparing the Center

1. Using the pattern on page 99, prepare the shoebox following the directions on page 55.

2. Laminate and cut out the task cards on pages 101, 103, and 105.

3. Reproduce a supply of answer forms on page 98. Place them next to the shoebox.

Using the Center

1. The student removes the cards from the leaf shoebox, selects a caterpillar, and writes its word on the answer form.

2. The student finds the two leaves that contain synonyms for the word on the caterpillar and writes them on the correct leaf on the answer form. The student should continue until the answer form is complete.

huge

big

large

Name _____

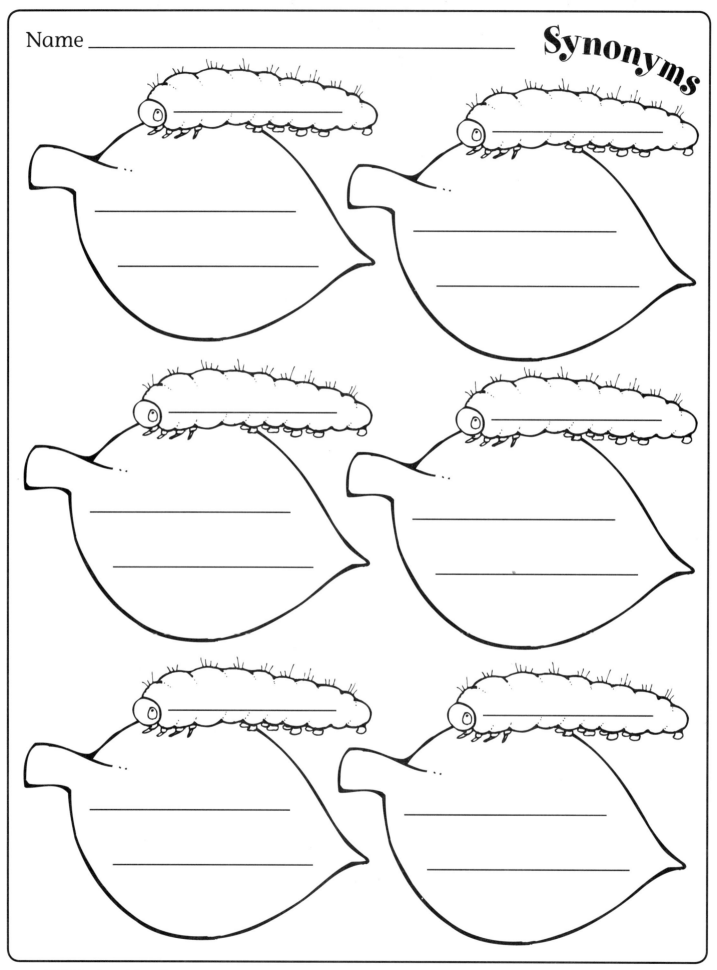

Synonyms

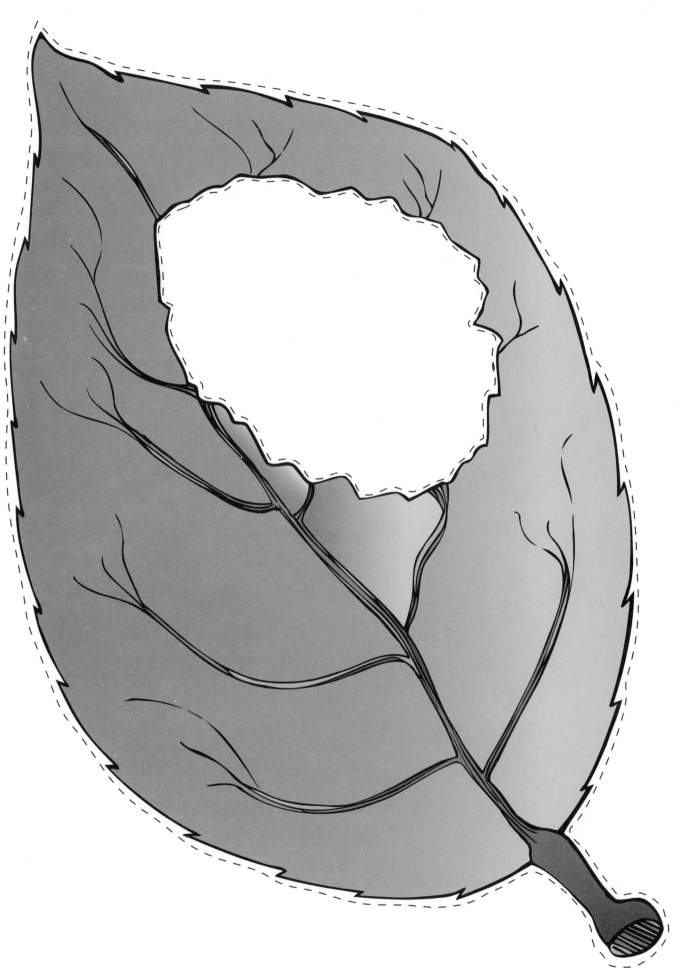

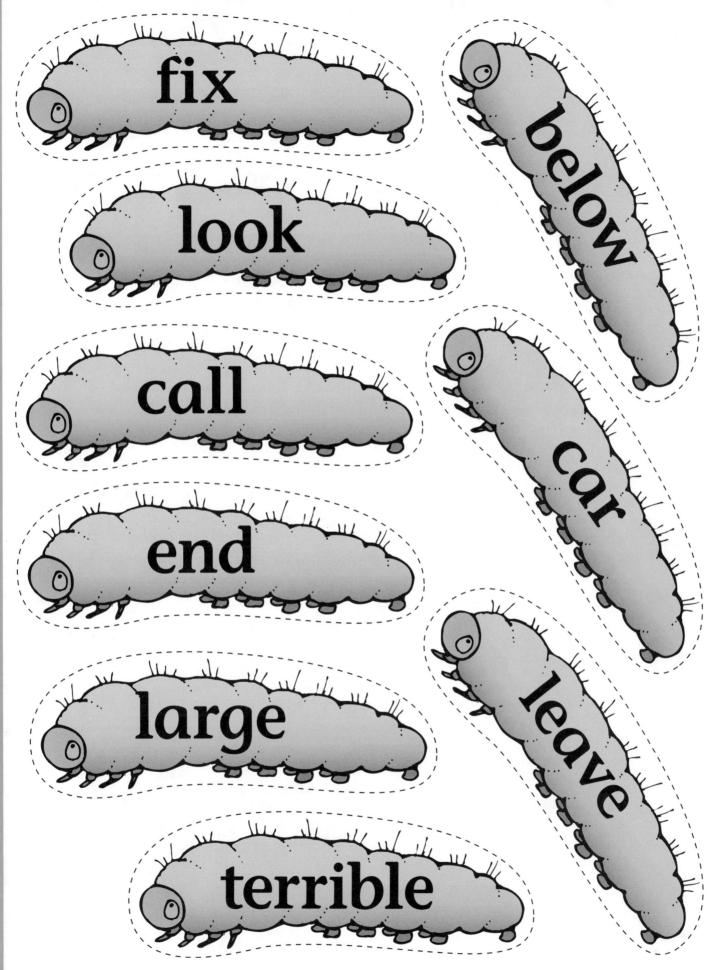

fix

below

look

call

car

end

large

leave

terrible

Literacy Centers - Take It to Your Seat • EMC 788

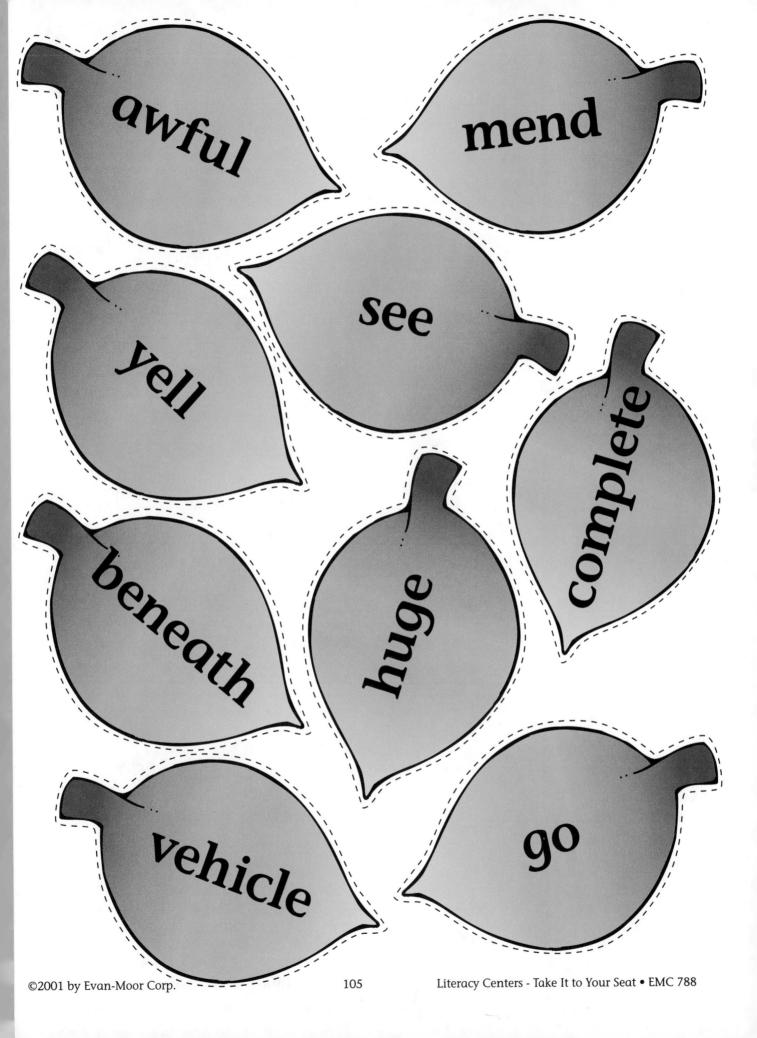

awful

mend

yell

see

complete

beneath

huge

vehicle

go

Rhyming

Glue the flower to the box lid.

Cut a hole in the lid.

too

Put flowers and bees inside the box.

do

blue

zoo

Preparing the Center

1. Using the pattern on page 109, prepare the shoebox following the directions on page 55.

2. Laminate and cut apart the task cards on pages 111, 113, 115, and 117.

3. Reproduce a supply of answer forms on page 108. Place them next to the shoebox.

bee

Using the Center

1. The student selects a flower from the flower shoebox and writes its word on the answer form.

2. The student removes the bees from the flower box, selects the bees that rhyme with the word on the flower, and then writes the rhyming words on the answer form. The student should continue until the answer form is complete.

sea

Rhyming

Cut out.

Literacy Centers - Take It to Your Seat • EMC 788

we

bee

tree

flea

she

pea

sea

111

fly

cry

tie

sky

pie

high

buy

go

so

sew

hoe

row

dough

blow

Literacy Centers - Take It to Your Seat • EMC 788

too

you

zoo

new

do

shoe

blue

 Literacy Centers - Take It to Your Seat • EMC 788

Folder Centers

Folder centers are easily stored in a box or file crate. Students take a folder to their desks to complete the task.

Making Folder Centers

Materials

- folders with pockets
- marking pens
- glue
- cellophane tape

Steps to Follow

1. Laminate and cut out the cover picture. Glue it to the front of the folder.

2. Tape the edge of the pockets closed as shown.

3. Place answer forms, writing paper, and any other supplies in the left-hand pocket.

4. Place task cards or envelopes in the right-hand pocket.

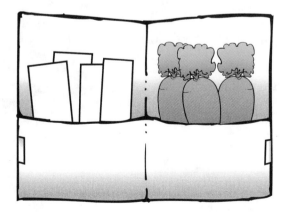

Antonyms

answer form

task cards

Preparing the Center

1. Prepare a folder following the directions on page 119. Laminate and cut out the pattern on page 123. Attach it to the front of the folder.

2. Laminate and cut out the task cards on pages 125 and 127. Place them in the right-hand pocket of the folder. (Page 122 provides blank cards for your own tasks.)

3. Reproduce a supply of the answer forms on page 121. Place them in the left-hand pocket of the folder.

Using the Center

1. The student matches the penguins containing antonyms.

2. Then the student writes the antonyms on the answer form.

hot

cold

1. _____

2. _____

3. _____

4. _____

5. _____

6. _____

7. _____

8. _____

1. _____

2. _____

3. _____

4. _____

5. _____

6. _____

7. _____

8. _____

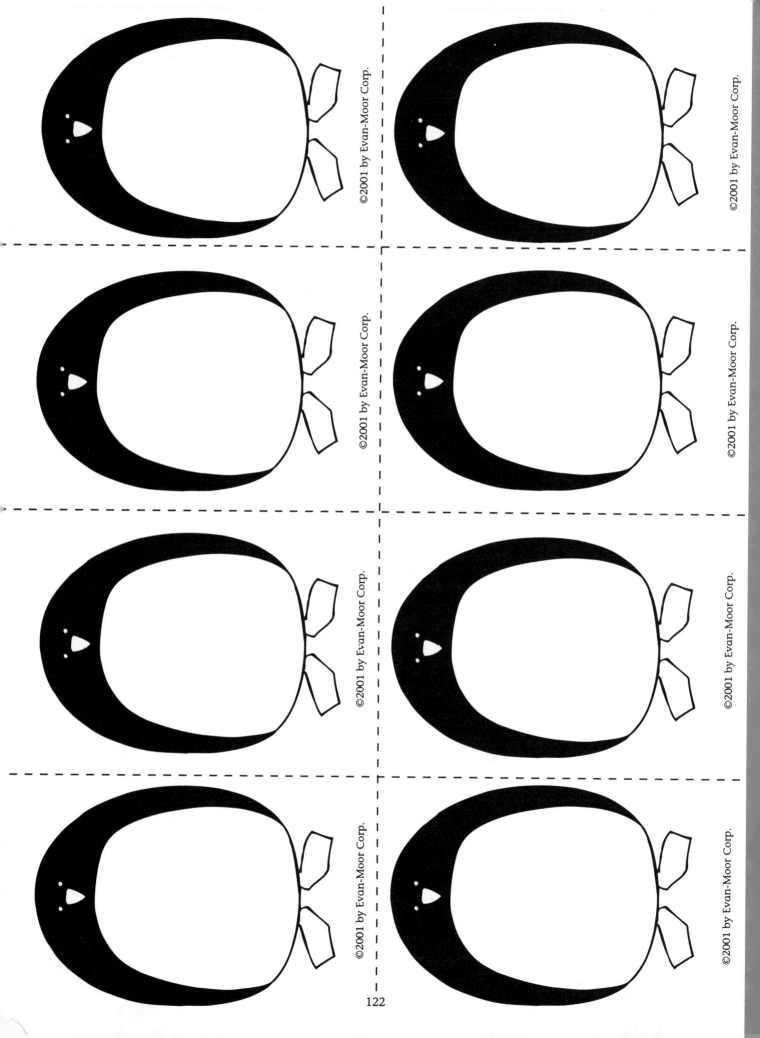

Antonyms

 Literacy Centers - Take It to Your Seat • EMC 788

Literacy Centers - Take It to Your Seat • EMC 788

straight

fix

crooked

break

depart

friend

arrive

stranger

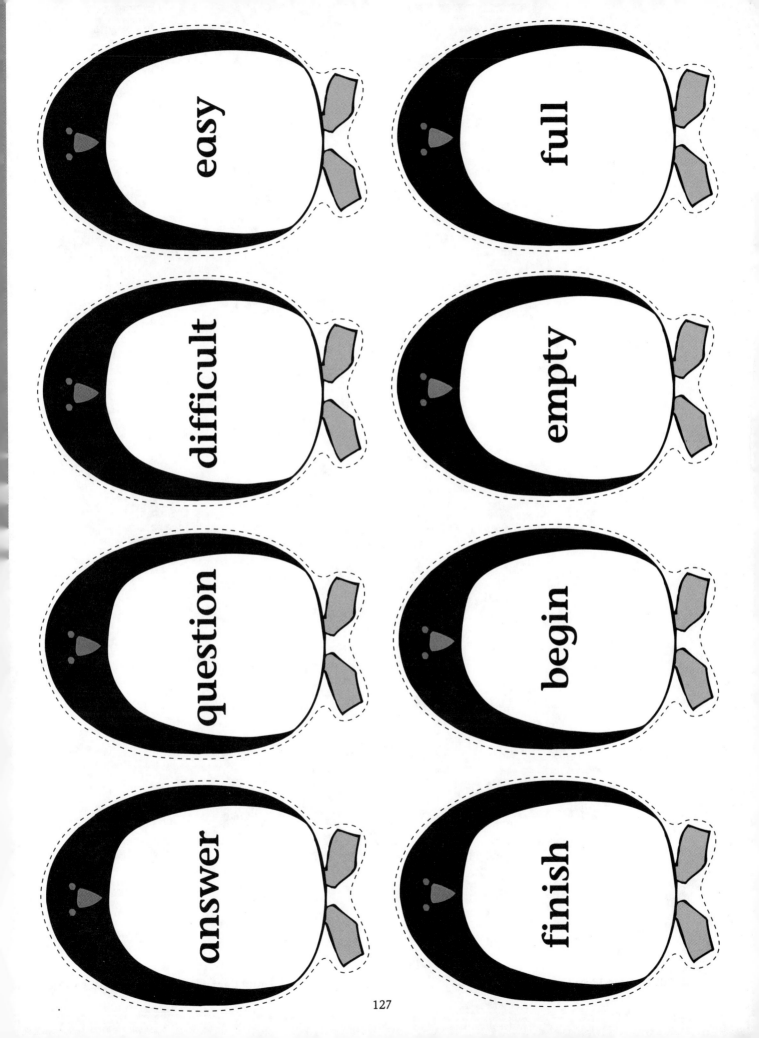

easy

full

difficult

empty

question

begin

answer

finish

Literacy Centers - Take It to Your Seat • EMC 788

Making Words

answer form

task cards

Preparing the Center

1. Prepare a folder following the directions on page 119. Laminate and cut out the pattern on page 131. Attach it to the front of the folder.

2. Laminate and cut apart the task cards on pages 133, 135, 137, and 139. Place them in the right-hand pocket of the folder.

3. Reproduce a supply of the answer forms on page 130. Place them in the left-hand pocket of the folder.

Using the Center

1. The student takes a cab card and then reads the trailer cards to find an ending to "hitch" to the cab to make a real word. (Some sounds may be used in more than one way.)

2. The student copies each word he or she makes on the answer form.

Making Words

Words I Made

1. _____

2. _____

3. _____

4. _____

5. _____

6. _____

7. _____

8. _____

9. _____

10. _____

11. _____

12. _____

13. _____

14. _____

15. _____

16. _____

Making Words

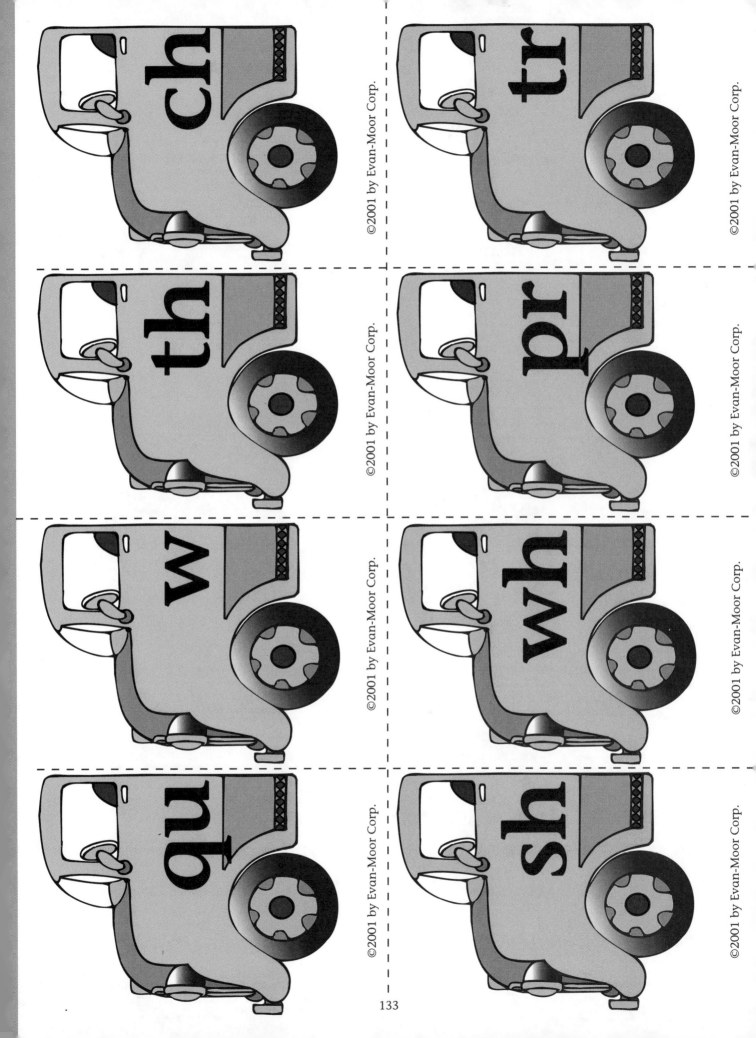

ch

th

w

qu

tr

pr

wh

sh

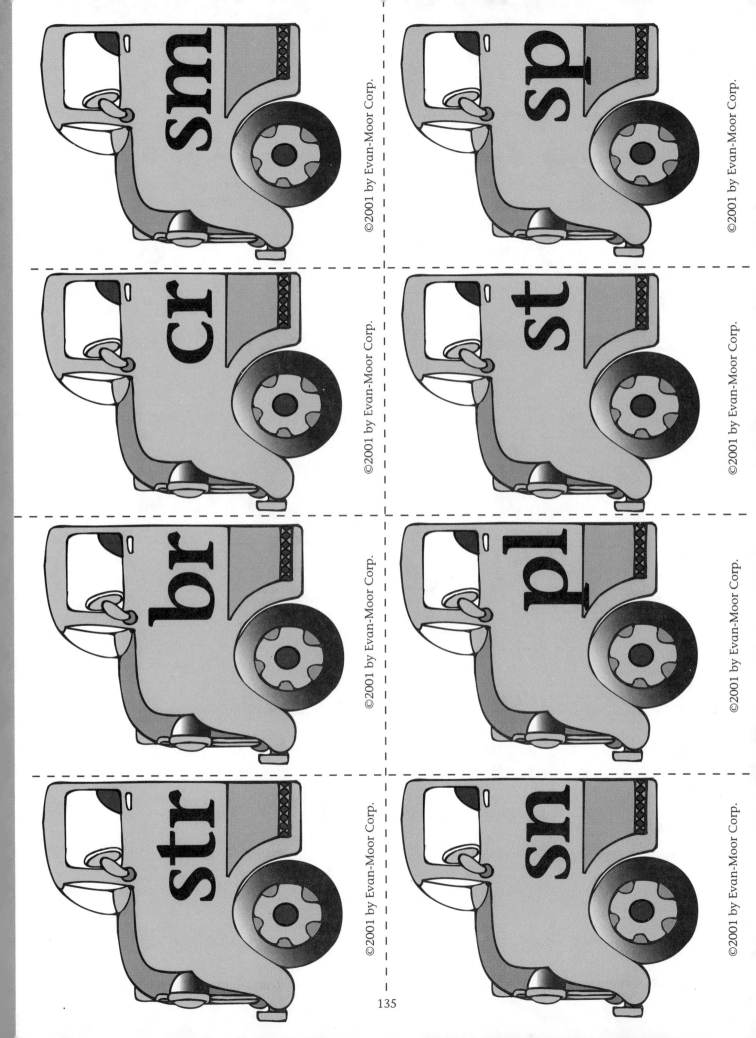

sm

sp

cr

st

br

pl

str

sn

air

ain

ree

etty

ater

en

een

ut

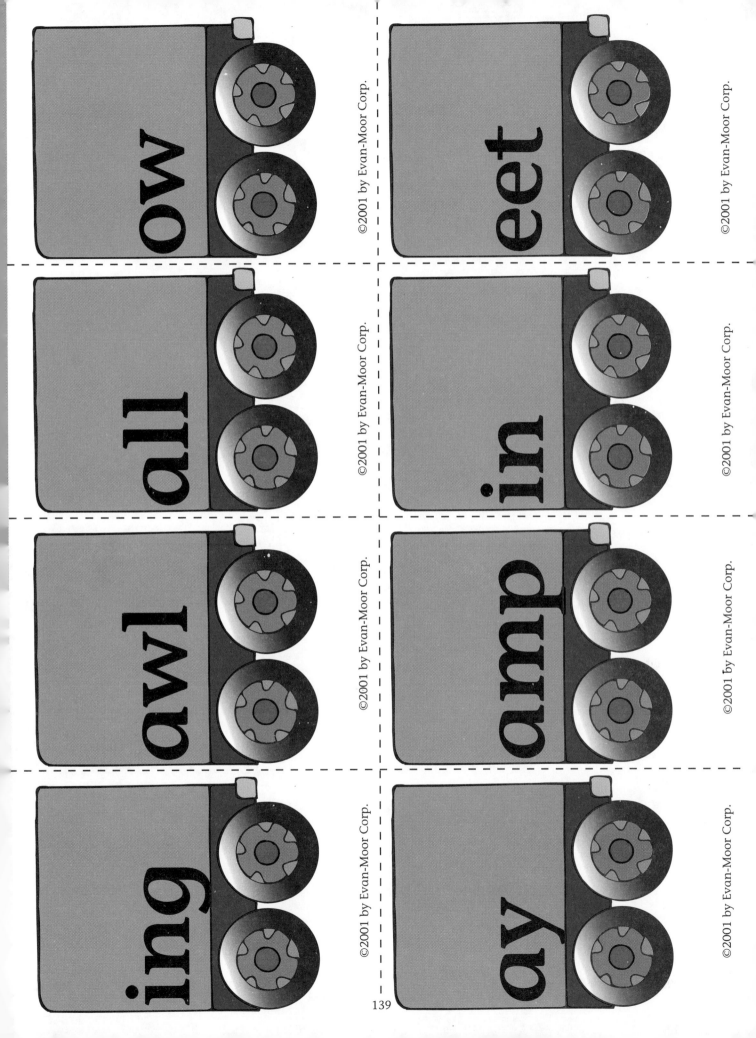

ow

all

awl

ing

eet

in

amp

ay

Singular or Plural?

answer form

task cards

Preparing the Center

1. Prepare a folder following the directions on page 119. Laminate and cut out the pattern on page 143. Attach it to the front of the folder.

2. Laminate and cut out the signs on page 145. Glue one sign to each folder pocket.

3. Laminate and cut out the task cards on pages 147, 149, 151, and 153. Place them in the right-hand pocket of the folder.

4. Reproduce a supply of the answer forms on page 142. Place them in the left-hand pocket of the folder.

Using the Center

1. The student sorts the cards into two sets—singular and plural, placing the cards in the correctly labeled pocket.

2. Then the student takes one set at a time and writes the words in the correct columns on the answer form.

Name _____   Singular or Plural?

Singular

Plural

1. _____   1. _____

2. _____   2. _____

3. _____   3. _____

4. _____   4. _____

5. _____   5. _____

6. _____   6. _____

7. _____   7. _____

8. _____   8. _____

Singular or Plural?

143

Singular

Plural

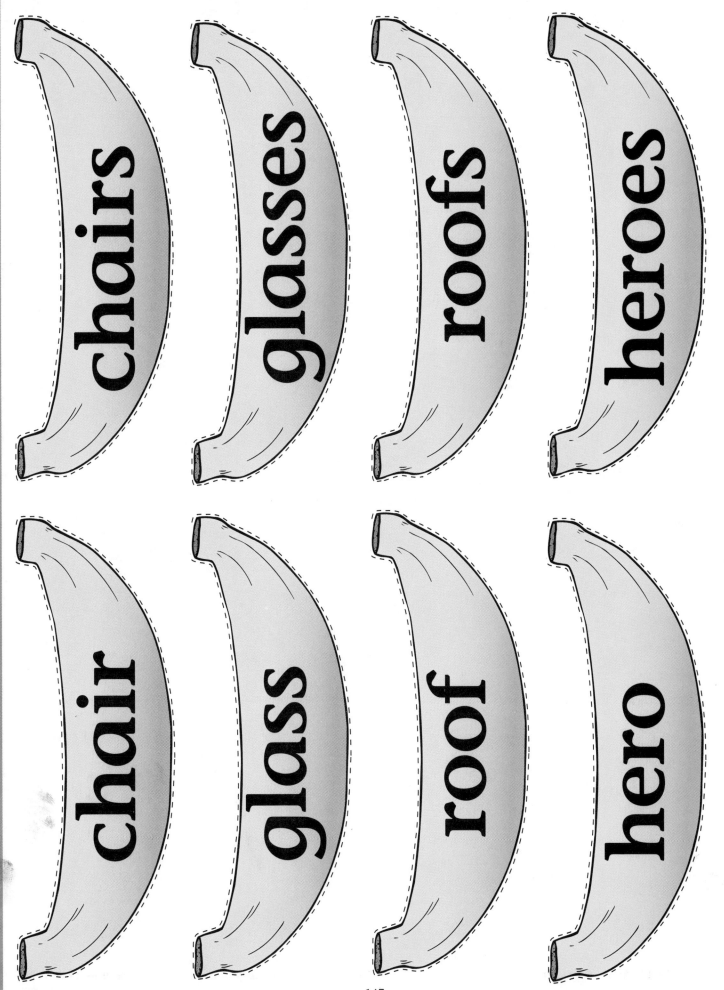

chairs

glasses

roofs

heroes

chair

glass

roof

hero

147

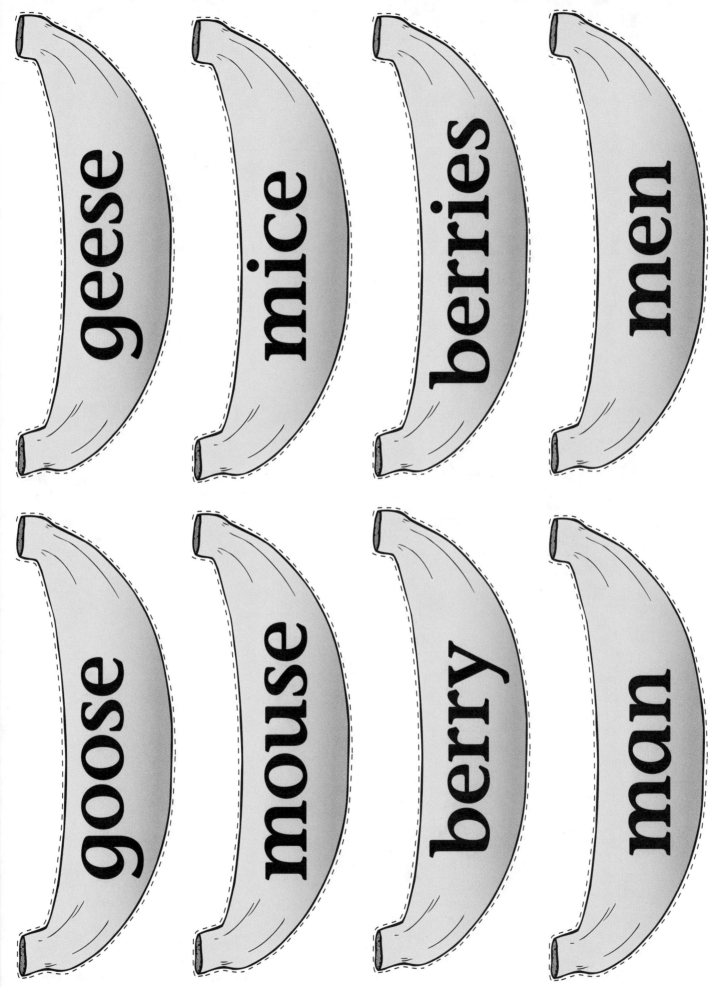

geese

mice

berries

men

goose

mouse

berry

man

149

women

children

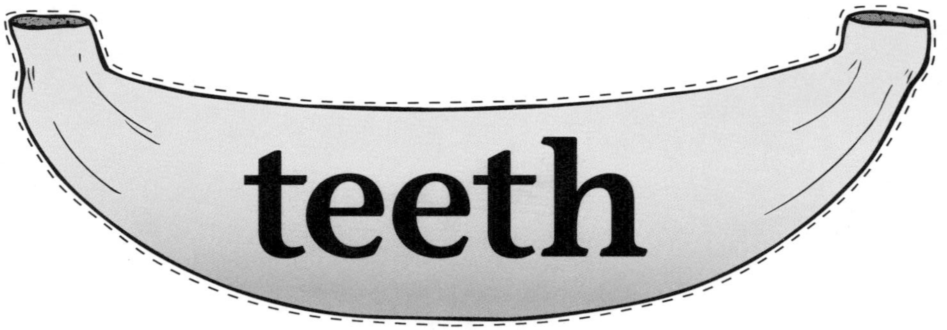

teeth

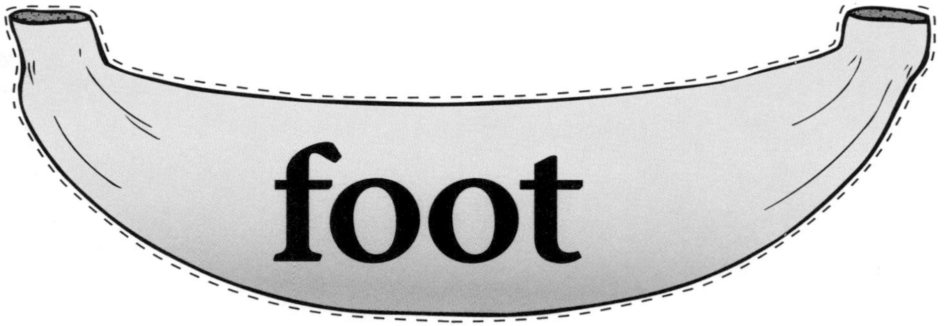

feet

woman

child

tooth

foot

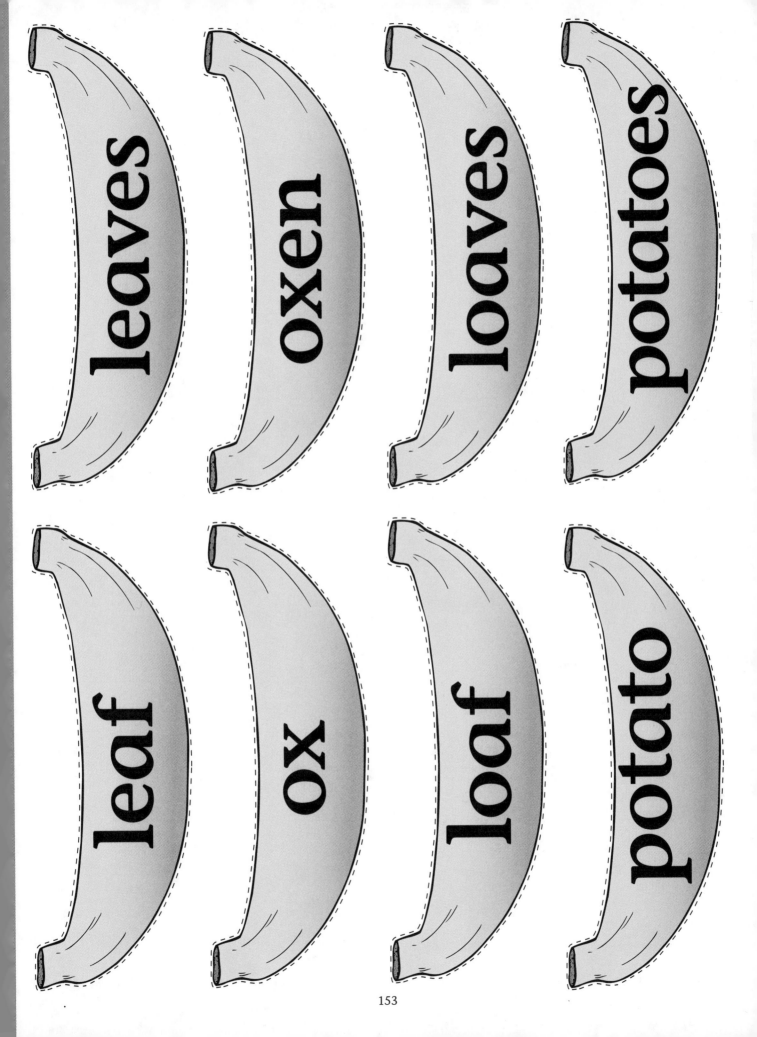

leaves

oxen

loaves

potatoes

leaf

ox

loaf

potato

153

Super Sentences

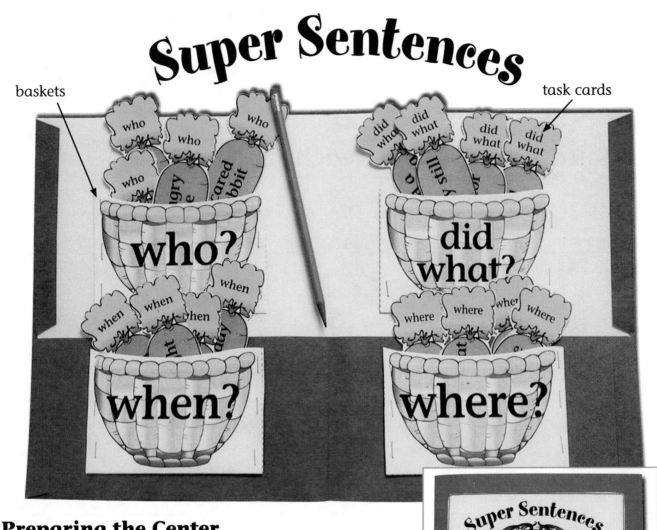

baskets

task cards

Preparing the Center

1. Prepare a folder following the directions on page 119. Laminate and cut out the pattern on page 157. Attach it to the front of the folder.

2. Laminate and cut out the task cards on pages 163, 165, 167, 169. Place them in the right-hand pocket of the folder.

3. Laminate and cut out pages 159 and 161. Fold and staple the sides to form "baskets." Tape the baskets inside the folder as shown above.

4. Reproduce a supply of the answer forms on page 156. Place them in the left-hand pocket of the folder.

Using the Center

1. The student sorts the carrot cards, placing them in the baskets labeled "who?" "did what?" "when?" and "where?"

2. The student chooses one carrot from each basket and uses the words to write a super sentence on the answer form. Repeat the process to write as many sentences as time allows.

Super Sentences

Take a carrot from each basket.
Write a super sentence.

Pick four new carrots for each sentence.

1. _____

_____

2. _____

_____

3. _____

_____

4 _____

_____

Super Sentences

 Literacy Centers - Take It to Your Seat • EMC 788

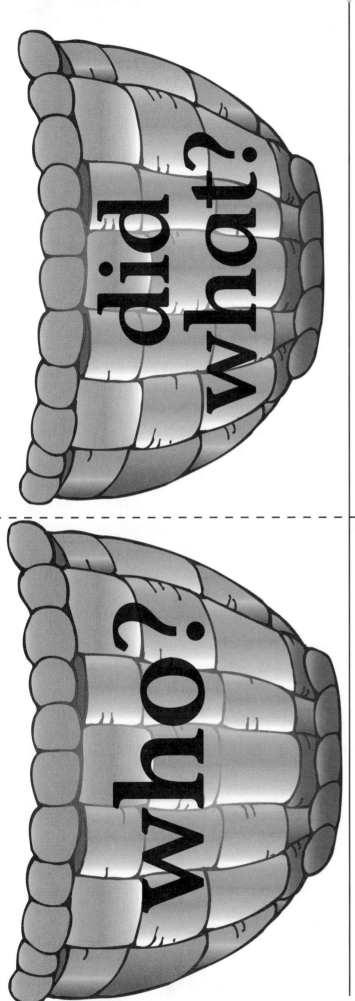

did? what?

who?

↑ Fold up to form pocket.

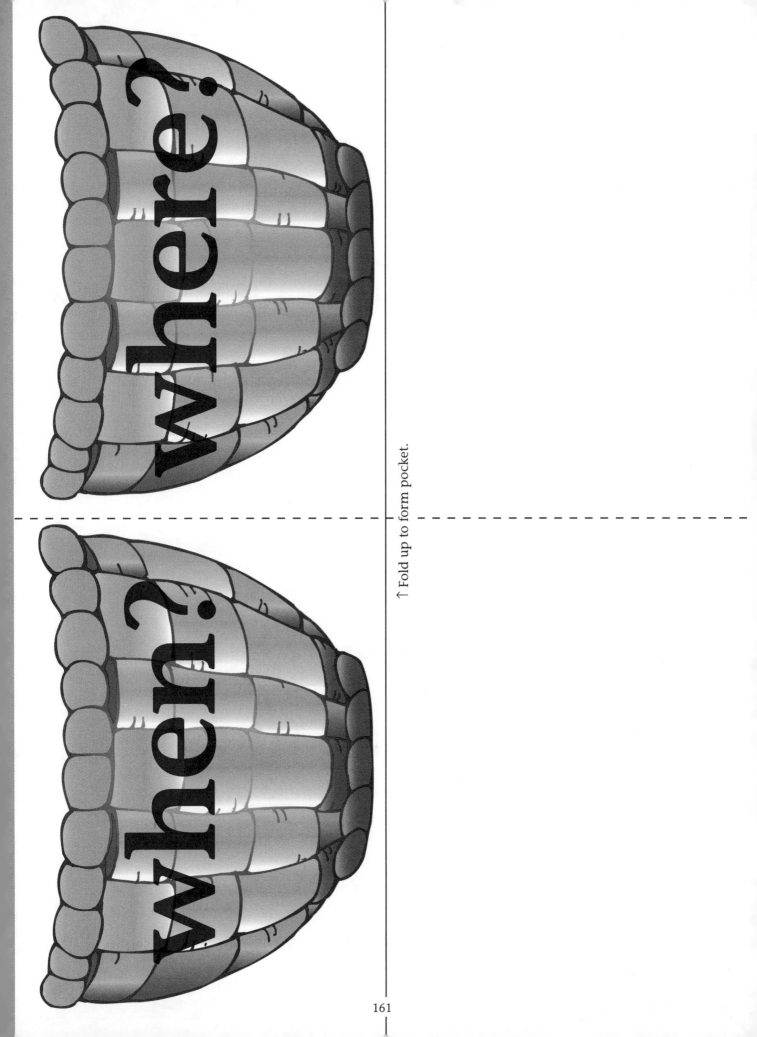

where?

when?

↑ Fold up to form pocket.

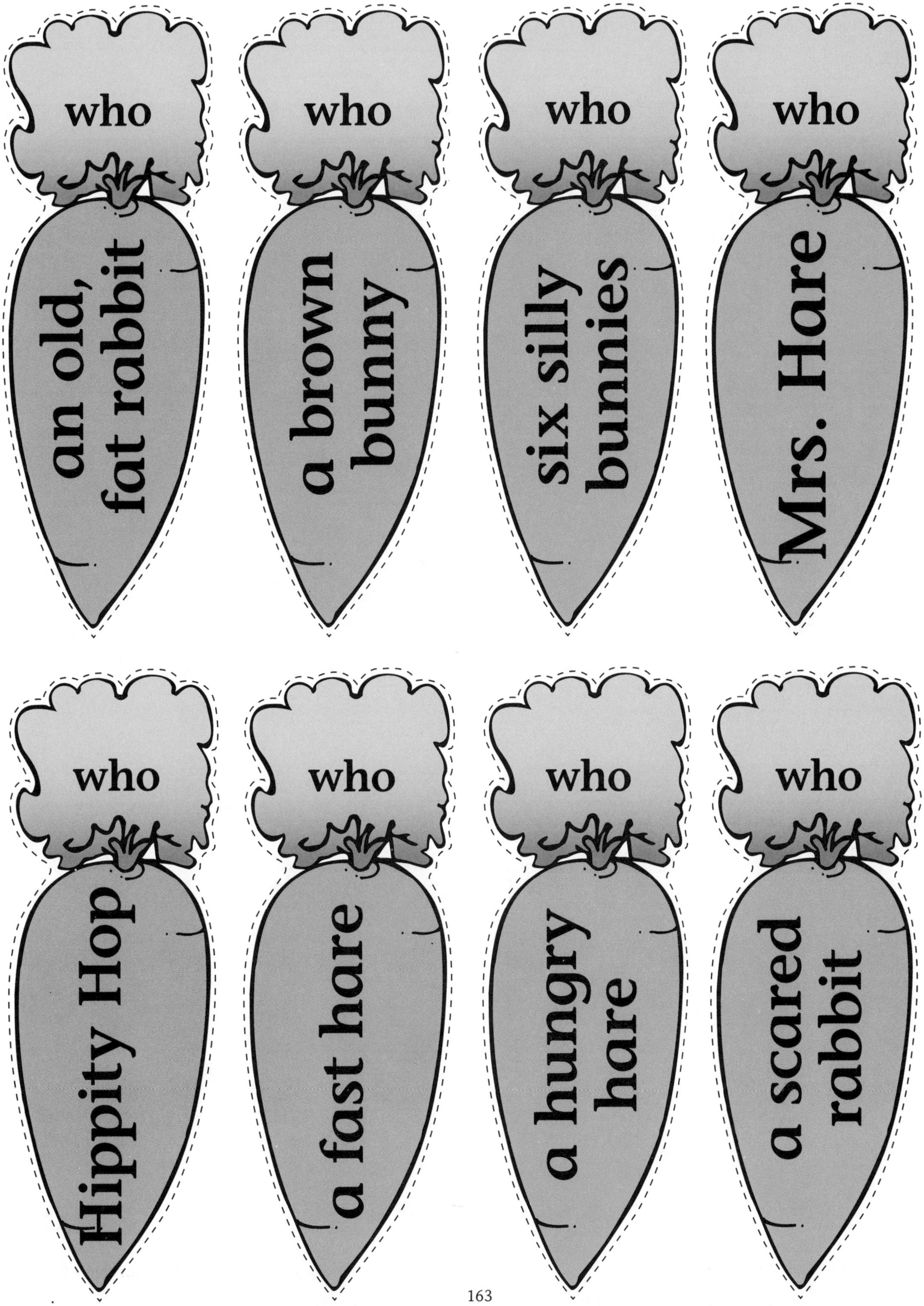

who

an old, fat rabbit

who

a brown bunny

who

six silly bunnies

who

Mrs. Hare

who

Hippity Hop

who

a fast hare

who

a hungry hare

who

a scared rabbit

did what

went to sleep

did what

hopped away

did what

nibbled grass

did what

grew bigger

did what

sat very still

did what

found a magic egg

did what

looked for food

did what

played

165

where

in a burrow

where

under the house

where

in the backyard

where

down a hole

where

in a meadow

where

behind that tree

where

at a pet shop

where

across the snow

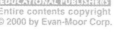

when

yesterday

when

all day long

when

in my dream

when

last night

when

before breakfast

when

as the sun came up

when

after the fox went away

when

just a minute ago

169

Alphabetical Order

answer form

envelopes with cards

task cards

Preparing the Center

1. Prepare a folder following the directions on page 119. Laminate and cut out the pattern on page 173. Attach it to the front of the folder.

2. Laminate and cut apart the task cards on pages 175, 177, and 179. Place each set in a separate envelope. Place them in the right-hand pocket of the folder.

3. Reproduce a supply of the answer forms on page 172. Place them in the left-hand pocket of the folder.

Using the Center

1. The student selects an envelope and puts the words inside in alphabetical order. (The task becomes more difficult in each succeeding envelope.)

2. The student writes the number of the task on the answer form, and then writes the words in order on the form.

Name _____ Set _____ **Alphabetical Order**

1. _____

2. _____

3. _____

4. _____

5. _____

6. _____

7. _____

8. _____

Name _____ Set _____ **Alphabetical Order**

1. _____

2. _____

3. _____

4. _____

5. _____

6. _____

7. _____

8. _____

Alphabetical Order

Literacy Centers - Take It to Your Seat • EMC 788

1

at

egg

cup

go

dog

fox

bat

hot

2

man

tell

pet

rat

off

next

queen

sun

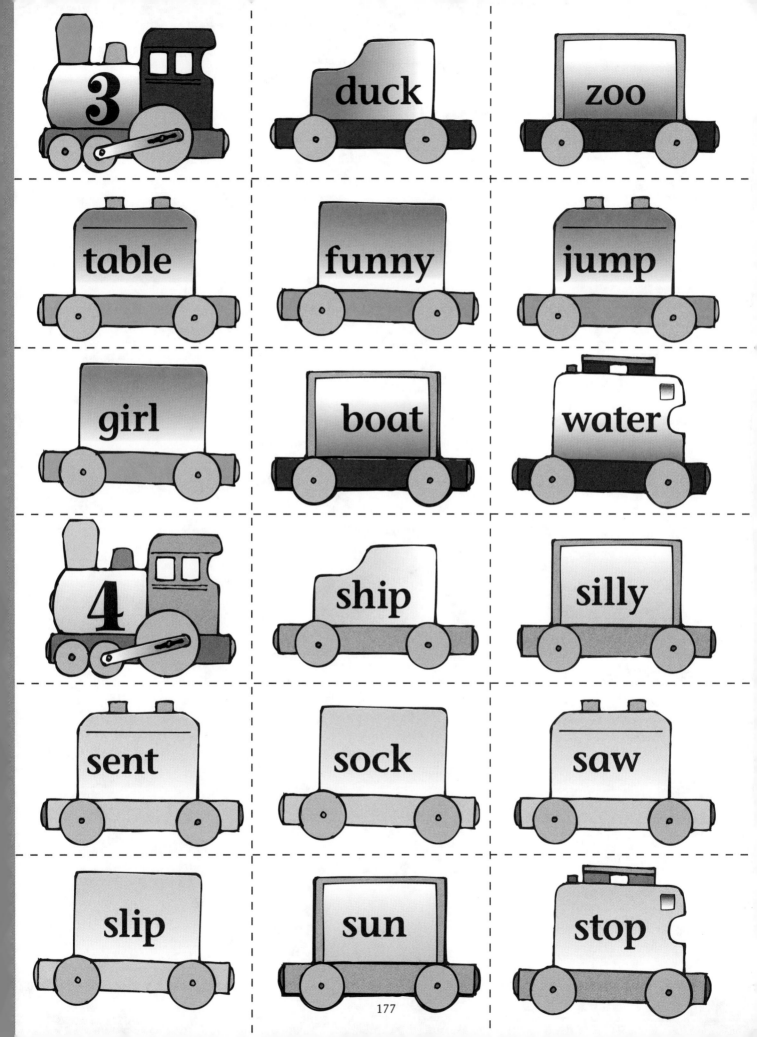

3

duck

zoo

table

funny

jump

girl

boat

water

4

ship

silly

sent

sock

saw

slip

sun

stop

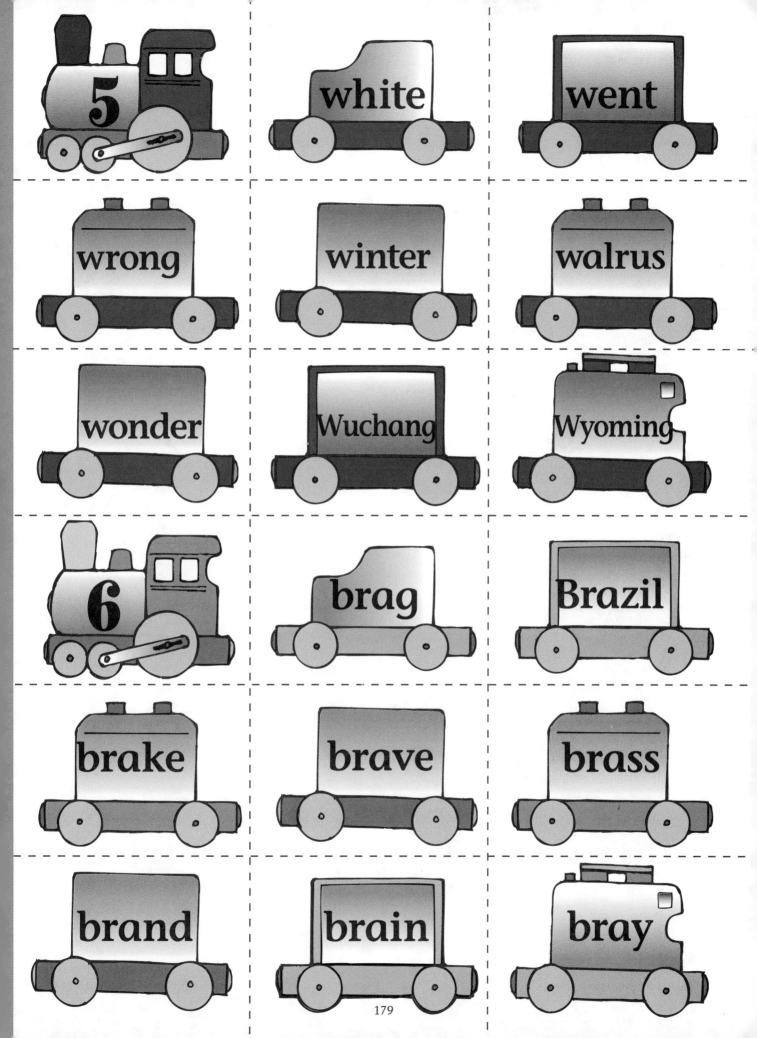

5

white

went

wrong

winter

walrus

wonder

Wuchang

Wyoming

6

brag

Brazil

brake

brave

brass

brand

brain

bray

179

Real or Make-Believe?

answer form

task cards

Preparing the Center

1. Prepare a folder following the directions on page 119. Laminate and cut out the pattern on page 185. Attach it to the front of the folder.

2. Laminate and cut out the signs on page 183. Glue them to the inside pockets.

3. Laminate and cut apart the task cards on pages 187, 189, and 191. Place them in the right-hand pocket of the folder.

4. Reproduce a supply of the answer forms on page 182. Place them in the left-hand pocket of the folder.

Using the Center

1. The student reads each card and decides if it describes something real or make-believe.

2. The student circles "real" or "make-believe" after the correct number on the answer form, and then places the card in the correct pocket of the folder.

1. real	make-believe	10. real	make-believe
2. real	make-believe	11. real	make-believe
3. real	make-believe	12. real	make-believe
4. real	make-believe	13. real	make-believe
5. real	make-believe	14. real	make-believe
6. real	make-believe	15. real	make-believe
7. real	make-believe	16. real	make-believe
8. real	make-believe	17. real	make-believe
9. real	make-believe	18. real	make-believe

Real

Make-Believe

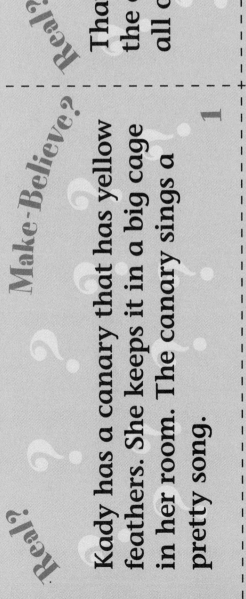

Real?   Make-Believe?

Kady has a canary that has yellow feathers. She keeps it in a big cage in her room. The canary sings a pretty song.

1

Make-Believe?   Real?

That greedy pig pushed all of the other pigs away. Then it ate all of the food in the trough.

2

Real?   Make-Believe?

Uncle Fred bought a big fat goose. When he got the goose home, he found that it could lay golden eggs.

3

Make-Believe?   Real?

Some ants carry seeds down into tunnels in the ground.

4

Real?   Make-Believe?

The mice had a meeting. "What are we going to do about that cat?" asked one little mouse.

5

Make-Believe?   Real?

Chondra found a large frog. She picked it up. Suddenly the frog spoke. "Kiss me and I will turn into a prince," it said. Chondra dropped the frog and ran home.

6

187

Literacy Centers - Take It to Your Seat • EMC 788

Real?   **Make-Believe?**

A monkey in a tree looked down and saw a crocodile swimming in the river.

7

Real?   **Make-Believe?**

A robin laid three eggs in her nest. She sat on the eggs until they hatched. Then she brought her babies food every day.

8

Real?   **Make-Believe?**

"Get out of those weeds, Candy!" Carlos shouted at his dog. "You will get stickers in your fur."

9

Real?   **Make-Believe?**

The wind blew Kelly's kite into a tree. She began to cry. Her father climbed the tree to get the kite. "We will fix your kite, Kelly," he said.

10

Real?   **Make-Believe?**

Amy opened her umbrella when the purple raindrops started to fall. "I don't want to get my hair wet," she said.

11

Real?   **Make-Believe?**

Mike's cat jumped up on the bed and patted Mike in the face. "Wake up, Mike. It's time to get ready for school," purred the cat.

12

Literacy Centers - Take It to Your Seat • EMC 788

Make-Believe? / Real?

14
Walter went fishing after school. The only thing he caught was an old boot that got stuck on his hook.

16
When Jack planted bean seeds in the yard, a giant beanstalk grew up into the sky. It reached all the way to the clouds.

18
A spaceship landed on the moon. Two men got out and walked on the moon. They brought moon rocks back to Earth.

13
Mr. Jacobs jumped into the water. He was searching for a ship that had sunk there. Mr. Jacobs had a map that showed where the ship had gone down. He hoped to find treasure on the ship.

15
Jed and Ralph were old horses. They couldn't work anymore. Their owner put the horses in the pasture. Now they could eat and rest all day.

17
I found a Leprechaun's pot of gold at the end of the rainbow.

©2001 by Evan-Moor Corp.

Literacy Centers - Take It to Your Seat • EMC 788